NUCLEAR TERRORISM AFTER 9/11

ROBIN M. FROST

ADELPHI PAPER 378

First published December 2005
by **Routledge**
4 Park Square, Milton Park, Abingdon, Oxon, OX14 4RN
for **The International Institute for Strategic Studies**
Arundel House, 13–15 Arundel Street, Temple Place, London, WC2R 3DX
www.iiss.org

Simultaneously published in the USA and Canada
by **Routledge**
270 Madison Ave., New York, NY 10016

Routledge is an imprint of the Taylor & Francis Group

© 2005 The International Institute for Strategic Studies

Director John Chipman
Editor Tim Huxley
Manager for Editorial Services Ayse Abdullah
Copy Editor Matthew Foley
Production Jesse Simon
Cover Image Lawrence Lawry/Getty Images

Typeset by Techset Composition Ltd, Salisbury, Wiltshire
Printed and bound in Great Britain by Bell & Bain Ltd, Thornliebank, Glasgow

British Library Cataloguing in Publication Data
A catalogue record for this book is available from the British Library

Library of Congress Cataloguing in Publication Data

ISBN 0-415-39992-0
ISSN 0567-932X

Contents

'If a 10-kiloton nuclear weapon, a midget even smaller than the one that destroyed Hiroshima, exploded in Times Square, the fireball would reach tens of millions of degrees Fahrenheit. It would vaporize or destroy the theater district, Madison Square Garden, the Empire State Building, Grand Central Terminal and Carnegie Hall ... The blast would partly destroy a much larger area, including the United Nations. On a weekday some 500,000 people would be killed. Could this happen? Unfortunately, it could – and many experts believe that such an attack, somewhere, is likely.'

Nicholas D. Kristof, 'An American Hiroshima',
New York Times, 11 August 2004.

'The bottom line is this: For the foreseeable future, the United States and other nations will face an existential threat *from the intersection of terrorism and weapons of mass destruction'* [emphasis added].

Senator Richard Lugar,
'Lugar Releases New Report on
WMD Threats and Responses', press release,
Office of Senator Richard Lugar, 22 June 2005.

'Sometimes it seems as if the source of newly announced dangers must be the basement of the White House or a back room at a Washington think tank, where the thousands of monkeys who have yet to type out exact copies of the works of Shakespeare are nonetheless producing dozens of new ideas for attacks on America, to be trotted out on the news at 10.'

Linda Rothstein, Catherine Auer and Jonas Siegel,
'Rethinking Doomsday',
Bulletin of the Atomic Scientists,
November–December 2004, pp. 36–41.

Introduction

This paper takes a position that runs counter to the views on nuclear terrorism expressed by many politicians and academics, as well as the media. It argues that the risk of nuclear terrorism, especially true nuclear terrorism employing bombs powered by nuclear fission, is overstated, and that popular wisdom on the topic is significantly flawed. There are technical, psychological and strategic grounds for this assertion, and the paper will deal with each of these categories in turn. At the same time, there are good reasons for concern about the state of nuclear security worldwide, and nothing in this paper should be read as suggesting that there is any cause for complacency. Far from it: serious efforts are required to improve the situation. Radioactive materials, and potential targets of nuclear terrorism, such as reactor complexes, must be better protected.

A set of implicit or explicit assumptions about nuclear terrorism underlies a good deal of the current discourse on the topic. Some of the key assumptions are given below. All of these assumptions are questionable, and several are simply false. The point Karl-Heinz Kamp made nine years ago applies just as well today: if all these assumptions were true, why is that terrorists still do not possess nuclear explosive devices?[1]

- The Russian nuclear arsenal, inherited from the Soviet Union, is so poorly secured that it has become an enormous 'Nukes-R-Us', staffed by a corrupt, demoralised and underpaid military, and patronised by terrorists and their criminal henchmen.

- There is a thriving international black market in nuclear weapons and materials.
- The plans and technical information necessary to build a functional nuclear weapon are widely available.
- Some so-called rogue states, especially Pakistan and North Korea (or entities within them), are willing to give or sell nuclear weapons to terrorists, if they have not already done so.
- The greatest potential threat is from terrorists using true nuclear weapons, but 'dirty bombs' could also be extremely dangerous, especially if they use substances such as uranium or plutonium.
- All terrorists, but most especially the anti-Western *jihadist* Islamist groups generically known as al-Qaeda, are irrational, mentally-ill killers who engage in terrorism to satisfy their bloodlust.
- As a corollary to the above, terrorists are uniformly eager to obtain, and willing to use, any and all weapons of mass destruction (WMD), including nuclear weapons.
- Nuclear terrorism constitutes an 'existential threat' to the United States and other potential target states.

In brief, the rebuttals to these assumptions can be put as follows.

- *Russian nuclear weapons.* Russian nuclear weapons appear to be under the generally good control of élite troops. There is no evidence in open-source material that a single nuclear warhead, from any national arsenal or another source, has ever made its way into the world's illegal arms bazaars, let alone into terrorist hands. No actual or aspiring nuclear-weapon state has ever claimed to have nuclear weapons without also having all of the technical infrastructure necessary to produce them *ab initio*, although they could, if the 'loose nukes' arguments were sound, easily have bought a few on the black market. Even the extravagant sums sometimes mentioned as the alleged asking price for stolen weapons would be tiny fractions of the amount required to develop an indigenous nuclear-weapon capability, yet circumstances seem to have compelled states to choose the more expensive course.
- *The nuclear black market.* There is no evidence in the open-source literature of a true international black market in nuclear materials. Virtually all known cases of nuclear theft or smuggling have involved amateurs hoping for rich returns, despite the seeming absence of anyone interested in buying the material. To the extent that a market

exists, it is almost entirely driven by supply; there appears to be no true demand, except where the buyers were government agents running a sting. Organised crime, with one known exception, has not been involved in nuclear trafficking. Even the notorious A.Q. Khan network concentrated on nuclear technology, especially centrifuge uranium enrichment, rather than fissile materials, although there have been suggestions that Khan, a Pakistani nuclear engineer, sold uranium hexafluoride, the feedstock for enrichment, to Libya.

- *'Do-it-yourself' nuclear weapons.* It is most improbable that any terrorist group could become a do-it-yourself nuclear power: unlike rough conceptual outlines, the detailed plans and engineering drawings necessary to build a bomb are not easily available.[2] It would also be very difficult, if not effectively impossible, to acquire sufficient quantities of suitable fissile materials. The expertise and facilities required to build a functional bomb, even a crude one, are of a higher order than those possessed by any known terrorist organisation. Developing nuclear weapons requires state-level resources, and the process takes years.

- *Dirty bombs and radiation dispersal devices.* Dirty bombs (also known as radiation dispersal devices or RDDs), are unlikely to kill anyone immediately, except via the direct effects of the conventional explosives involved. Neither uranium nor plutonium is particularly radioactive in pure form, and the widespread belief that plutonium is the world's most toxic substance is an outright myth, although both metals are toxic to some degree. Other radioactive materials, such as cesium-137 or strontium-90, could be dangerous, although they might kill or disable any would-be dirty-bomb maker before they could complete their work. Depending on the substance used and the size of the radiation release, a RDD might cause a small statistical increase in cancer deaths among those affected, although it might never be possible to attribute individual deaths to the RDD. A large RDD using spent but still hot reactor fuel could be very dangerous. The economic, social and psychological effects of a dirty bomb could be considerably more serious than its physical or radiological effects.

- *State sponsors of nuclear terrorism.* Nuclear-weapon states, even 'rogues', are most unlikely to be foolish enough to hand nuclear weapons, which are among their dearest national treasures, over to such unreliable, unpredictable and potentially dangerous characters as terrorists, especially when the chances of a suspected state sponsor suffering nuclear retaliation and annihilation are so good, and so blindingly obvious.[3]

- *Psychotic terrorist killers.* The overwhelming majority of terrorists are as psychologically healthy, rational and intelligent as the rest of us; indeed, mentally ill terrorists would be far less dangerous and much easier to deal with. Terrorists are typically neither psychopathic nor psychotic, nor are they driven by mere bloodlust. Furthermore, terrorists have not historically been particularly interested in WMD, and no terrorist use of WMD of any kind has resulted in mass casualties, unless the airliners used in New York and Washington on 11 September 2001 ('9/11') count as weapons of mass destruction. States, on the other hand, have used WMD to great effect. This is not to say that terrorists are not interested in killing large numbers of people; clearly, some are. Much of the concern about nuclear terrorism derives from the reasonable fear that al-Qaeda might be planning an attack even more lethal than those of 9/11. However, neither al-Qaeda nor any of the organisations linked to it has ever used WMD, and the evidence that they have the will or technical capacity to do so is limited and unconvincing.

- *An existential threat.* When applied to nuclear terrorism, the phrase 'existential threat' implies that a state such as the United States could be destroyed by terrorists wielding nuclear weapons. Yet to destroy the United States or any other large industrial state, in the sense of inflicting such damage to its government, economy, population and infrastructure that it could no longer function as a coherent political and economic entity, would require a large number of well-placed nuclear weapons with yields in the tens or hundreds of kilotons. It is unlikely that terrorists could successfully obtain, emplace and detonate a single nuclear weapon, while no plausible radiological device or devices could do any significant damage on a national level.

These arguments do not mean that the possibility of true nuclear terrorism can be ignored. Even a minuscule risk is too high, given the nature of the threat. But fear of that most terrifying image, a terrorist with an atom bomb, should not blind us to the need to prevent and defend against the much more probable forms of nuclear terrorism: attacks on nuclear reactors or other elements of the nuclear fuel cycle, and RDDs powered by industrial or medical radiation sources. By the same token, for all the focus on *jihadist* Islamic terrorism, other groups might, under certain circumstances, be more dangerous.

CHAPTER ONE

The Nuclear Black Market

Nuclear terrorism constitutes neither a single entity nor a narrow category. Acts of nuclear terrorism could range from distributing harmless amounts of radioactive material by mail to the use of large and powerful RDDs, improvised nuclear devices (INDs) or even nuclear weapons appropriated from a state arsenal. Some forms of nuclear terrorism would do little or no physical harm; others could render cities uninhabitable or, in the worst case, kill people in their tens or even hundreds of thousands. The following is a rough hierarchy, from the lowest to the highest level of hazard. It is necessarily somewhat arbitrary, as the lethality of many events depends on a host of variables, some of them unknown and possibly even unknowable.

1. Theft or sabotage of nuclear items for demonstration or blackmail.
2. Environmental contamination – of a city's water supply, for example – with radioactive material.
3. Attack on a nuclear reactor or other facility to spread alarm, but with no significant release of radiation.
4. Capture of a nuclear reactor for purposes of blackmail.
5. Sabotage of a reactor, storage dump or other nuclear facility short of meltdown or a fuel fire.
6. A credible, widely publicised nuclear threat that proves to be a hoax (a difficult item to rank, as its effects could in some respects be similar to a genuine attack).
7. Detonation of a RDD.

8. Damage to a spent fuel storage pool causing a fuel fire.
9. Detonation of a low-yield IND.
10. Damage to a nuclear reactor including core meltdown, containment breach and large-scale radiation release.
11. Detonation of a nuclear weapon from a state arsenal.[1]

Almost every kind of nuclear terrorism begins with access to radioactive materials: without nuclear or radioactive materials, there can be (almost) no nuclear terrorism. This chapter considers the threats posed by 'loose' radioactive materials, from radioactive scrap to nuclear weapons, and the putative black market in which they are traded.

The International Atomic Energy Agency (IAEA)'s Illicit Trafficking Database (ITDB) is probably the most authoritative source on the topic, although there are others, including the Stanford Database on Nuclear Smuggling, Theft, and Orphan Radiation Sources (SDTO).[2] The ITDB defines 'trafficking' very broadly, to include the 'unauthorized acquisition, provision, possession, use, transfer, or disposal of nuclear material and other radioactive material, whether intentional or unintentional and with or without crossing international borders. It also includes unsuccessful or thwarted events and incidents involving the inadvertent loss of control of nuclear and other radioactive materials and the discovery of such uncontrolled materials'.[3] The database also covers the broadest possible range

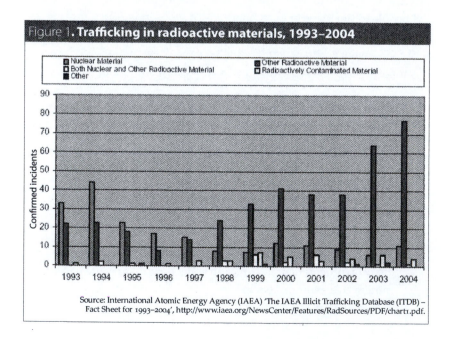

Figure 1. **Trafficking in radioactive materials, 1993–2004**

Source: International Atomic Energy Agency (IAEA) 'The IAEA Illicit Trafficking Database (ITDB) – Fact Sheet for 1993–2004', http://www.iaea.org/NewsCenter/Features/RadSources/PDF/chart1.pdf.

of radioactive materials, including substances merely contaminated with radiation ('radioactive junk').

Figure 1 shows that trafficking in nuclear material peaked in 1994, but had declined to a steady level of around ten incidents a year by 1998. The majority of incidents involved natural uranium, depleted uranium or low-enriched uranium (LEU) reactor fuel (which is not weapons usable). Some episodes of theft and diversion of LEU have involved very large amounts. For example, in 1993 a metalworker at the Electrostal reactor-fuel manu-facturing plant in Moscow Oblast diverted 115kg of uranium dioxide pellets, apparently because he was desperate for money to support his family, having not been paid for months.[4] In 1992, an entire nuclear reactor fuel assembly containing more than 100kg of LEU was apparently driven out of the Ignalina nuclear-power plant in Lithuania tied to the bottom of a bus.[5] Media reports concerning the fate of the material appeared sporadi-cally over the next few years.[6]

Twenty confirmed incidents have involved highly enriched uranium (HEU)[7] or plutonium-239 (Pu^{239});[8] these are listed in Table 1. According to the IAEA, most 'featured very small quantities'.[9] As of December 2004 (the most recent year for which the agency has released complete data), no trafficking incident known to the IAEA involved more than a very small fraction of the quantity required to build a weapon, and the number of those that have involved true weapons-grade fissile materials is debatable.[10] The total for all IAEA-confirmed trafficking cases involv-ing HEU for the decade from 1993 to 2003 was just 8.35kg. Even if it had all been weapons-grade material *and* all in one shipment, this would still have been about two-thirds short of the 25kg of HEU required for a basic bomb.[11] With the notable exception of 363g of mixed plutonium–uranium oxide (MOX) reactor fuel seized at Munich airport in Germany in 1994, the quantities of plutonium known to have been trafficked have been minute.[12] The largest single haul of pure plutonium was a tiny pellet of extremely highly enriched, 'super-grade' metal seized at Tengen in Germany in 1994.[13] The source of the substance remains unknown, although there are suspicions that it came from a Soviet weapons labora-tory. The total amount of IAEA-confirmed plutonium trafficked between 1993 and 2003 was 374.3g, or less than one-twelfth of the amount needed for a basic bomb.

According to the Russian Analytical Center for Non-Proliferation, the Landshut and Munich airport events, as well as an incident in Moscow in May 1995 involving 1.7kg of HEU (possibly the same one listed by the IAEA as taking place in June 1995) were the result of law-enforcement stings.[14]

Table 1. IAEA-confirmed incidents involving HEU or Pu, 1993–2004

Date	Location	Material involved	Incident description
24/5/1993	Vilnius, Lithuania	HEU, 150g	4.4 tons of beryllium including 140kg contaminated with HEU were discovered in the storage area of a bank. Beryllium was imported legally.
March 1994	St Petersburg, Russia	HEU, 2.972kg	An individual was arrested in possession of HEU, which he had stolen from a nuclear facility for sale.
10/5/1994	Tengen-Wiechs, Germany	Pu, 6.2 g	The material was detected in a building during a police search.
13/6/1994	Landshut, Germany	HEU, 0.795g	Police arrested a group in illegal possession of HEU.
25/7/1994	Munich, Germany	Pu, 0.24g	A small sample of PuO_2–UO_2 mixture was confiscated in an incident related to a larger seizure at Munich airport.
10/8/1994	Munich airport, Germany	Pu, 363.4g	PuO_2–UO_2 mixture was seized at Munich airport.
14/12/1994	Prague, Czech Republic	HEU, 2.73kg	HEU was seized by police in Prague.
June 1995	Moscow, Russia	HEU, 1.7kg	An individual was arrested in possession of HEU stolen from a nuclear facility.
6/6/1995	Prague, Czech Republic	HEU, 0.415g	An HEU sample was seized by police in Prague.
8/6/1995	Ceske Budejovice, Czech Republic	HEU, 16.9g	An HEU sample was seized by police in Ceske Budejovice.
29/5/1999	Rousse, Bulgaria	HEU, 10g	Customs officials arrested a man trying to smuggle HEU at the Rousse customs border check point.
2/10/1999	Kara-Balta, Kyrgyzstan	Pu, 1.49g	Two individuals were arrested trying to sell Pu.
19/4/2000	Batumi, Georgia	HEU, 770g	Four individuals were arrested in possession of HEU.
16/9/2000	Tbilisi airport, Georgia	Pu, 0.4 g	Nuclear material including Pu was seized by police at Tbilisi airport.
December 2000	Karlsruhe, Germany	Pu, 0.001g	Mixed radioactive materials including a minute quantity of plutonium were stolen from a former pilot reprocessing plant.
28/1/2001	Asvestochori, Greece	Pu, ~3g	245 small metal plates containing Pu were found in a buried cache in the Kouri forest near the village of Asvestochori.
16/7/2001	Paris, France	HEU, 0.5g	Three individuals trafficking in HEU were arrested in Paris. The perpetrators were seeking buyers for the material.
28/01/2001	Asvestochori, Greece	Pu~3 g	245 small metal plates containing Pu were found in a buried cache in the Kouri forest near the Asvestochori village.
16/07/2001	Paris, France	HEU 0.5 g	Three individuals trafficking in HEU were arrested in Paris. The perpetrators were seeking buyers for the material.
26/03/2003	Sadahlo, Georgia	HEU ~170 g	An individual was arrested attempting to illegally transport HEU across the border.

Source: IAEA Illicit Trafficking Database 'List of Confirmed Incidents Involving HEU or Pu', http://www.iaea.org/NewsCenter/Features/RadSources/PDF/table1.pdf.

The only incident that may have involved enough nuclear material to make a bomb apparently took place in 1998 in Chelyabinsk Oblast in Russia, and reportedly involved 18.5kg of radioactive material. The case remains unclear, however. Although the US Central Intelligence Agency (CIA) has twice reported an incident in Chelyabinsk,[15] the National Intelligence Council (NIC)'s 2004 *Annual Report to Congress on the Safety and Security of Russian Nuclear Facilities and Military* stated that the Russian security services had prevented the theft, so the material never actually left the grounds.[16] It also remains unclear whether the material in question was weapons-grade Pu, HEU or a precursor, such as natural or low-enriched uranium.

Since it was apparently thwarted, the Chelyabinsk incident does not appear on the IAEA list. Several other incidents which took place before the establishment of the Illicit Trafficking Database in 1995 are also not covered. William C. Potter claims that one of the earliest known cases of HEU theft took place in July 1993 at the Andreeva Guba naval base in Russia, not far from the Norwegian border. Two Russian sailors stole 1.8kg of 36%-enriched HEU from two submarine fuel assemblies. In a similar incident, in November 1993, a retired naval captain and an accomplice are said to have broken into a fuel-storage area at the Sevmorput shipyard near Murmansk, stealing 4.5kg of 20%-enriched HEU.[17] US academic Rensselaer W. Lee claims that 7kg of HEU was stolen from the Sovietskaya Gavan naval base in Kaliningrad.[18] It is unclear why these incidents have not been confirmed by the IAEA, while others from the same period have been. In any case, the materials involved were not weapons-usable, except perhaps by a very advanced national programme, and the quantities involved were far short of the amount required for bombs. Traffic in 'other radioactive material', mostly sealed radioactive sources containing various isotopes, as well as radioactive junk, has shown a striking increase from 1996 to 2004. However, according to the IAEA '[a] large portion of incidents involving radioactive sources did not evidence criminal activity. The Database has recorded numerous cases of discoveries of uncontrolled radioactive sources, often referred to as orphan sources.'[19]

The only known incident implicating organised crime involved reactor fuel. In 1998, a 19.9%-enriched, or very nearly highly enriched, reactor fuel element was seized in Italy from mafiosi trying to sell it, apparently to unnamed Middle Eastern countries. It is widely thought that the element was one of two fuel assemblies that went missing in the 1970s from a TRIGA research reactor in Congo (which is still operating under very poor security).[20] Speaking to a US Senate committee in 1996, then CIA director John Deutch stated that: 'We have no evidence ... that large organised crime groups with international connections are involved in the trafficking of radioactive materials'.[21] Lee quotes 'European police officials', spokesmen for Russia's internal security agencies and Russian Interpol as saying much the same thing.[22]

Comparisons are sometimes made between the drug trade and the illicit traffic in nuclear materials, the implication being that the detected traffic represents only a tiny fraction of the actual flow of goods. This argument is weak, although it cannot be completely dismissed. The huge demand for illegal drugs is obvious, but there is almost no evidence of a comparable demand for nuclear materials. To argue that a large black market exists, and that the failure to detect it is proof of the fiendish cunning of those who operate it, is sophistry of the least persuasive kind. Lee provided an excellent example in testimony to the US Congress Subcommittee on Prevention of Nuclear and Biological Attack in September 2005: 'Admittedly the visible face of the nuclear black market doesn't seem very compelling. Lots of radioactive junk floating around. A multitude of sellers, a few bona fide buyers, and some more a minor international nuisance than a first-order strategic threat. But this picture may be misleading. As with other illegal businesses – drugs, for example – what is seized is only a small fraction of what may be circulating in international smuggling channels.'[23] Lee went on to say that 'important incidents go unreported or undetected – actually go under-reported, especially in former Soviet bloc countries'. This is simply fatuous: if these incidents were unreported or undetected, Lee could not know about them or assert their existence. In the case of 'unreported' incidents, Lee might conceivably have access to classified information, although he made no such claim, but in the case of 'undetected' incidents, no one but the parties directly involved can know anything about them. Far from under-reporting, it may well be the case, as Deutch has pointed out, that incidents of nuclear trafficking in the former Soviet Union are in fact sensationalised or *over*-reported.[24] It is even possible that media coverage has to some extent created the problem of nuclear smuggling: 'For Smirnov [Leonid Smirnov, the first known thief of weapons-grade fissile material] and many other thieves, the idea of material diversion was prompted by extensive coverage by the mass media. Newspaper reports on nuclear trafficking raised the awareness about the value of such material, often exaggerated, among the general public and thus involuntarily contributed to the increased number of thefts.'[25]

Lee's further remark that 'sophisticated thieves and smugglers are less likely to get caught than the amateur players and scam artists who dominate the known smuggling incidents'[26] is self-evidently true but, again, it has nothing to say about the actual market and activities therein. No one, Lee included, has been able to provide, at least in the open sources, concrete evidence of *a single case* in which a substantial portion of the fissile materials needed to make a bomb had been, or was close to being, illicitly transferred to terrorists, organised criminals or, indeed, anyone actively seeking them. It is clearly possible that the actual black market is larger than the IAEA's database suggests – law enforcement is not perfect, after all – but it is not likely to be much larger: 'In sum, the visible manifest market for nuclear materials appears disorganised, chaotic, dominated by bumbling amateurs, and artificial in important respects; genuine buyers with real money seldom make an appearance, even in the few cases where weapons-usable materials are offered for sale ... Moreover ... the nuclear materials flowing through international smuggling channels frequently are nothing more than artifacts of undercover operations.'[27]

'Loose' Russian tactical nuclear weapons

'If you're Osama bin Laden and you want a nuclear weapon, where are you going? You're not going to Iraq, they don't have nuclear weapons. You're not going to Iran, they don't have nuclear weapons. You're not even going to North Korea. Even if they had them, are they going to give them up? Where is Osama bin Laden going to go? He's going to go to where the weapons are. To the Soviet Union, where there are 17,000. Where there's enough highly enriched uranium and fissile material for 40,000 more ... protected by a padlock and a guard that works during the day.'[28]

One of the more important sources of concern in the field of nuclear terrorism has been the disposition and security of the former Soviet Union's arsenal of tactical (that is, sub- or non-strategic) nuclear warheads. Commentators regularly raise the spectre of 'loose nukes' making their way from the Russian stockpile into the hands of terrorists, although they are seldom precise in their use of numbers. Thus: 'Strewn across Russia, there are tens of thousands of strategic nuclear weapons and components, thousands of small tactical nuclear weapons, and stores of fissile materials (plutonium or highly enriched uranium), which could be used to construct a crude nuclear bomb.'[29] Or this: 'Thousands of these arms are scattered throughout Russia, in the form of missile warheads, artillery shells, aircraft bombs and land mines. Because of the security weaknesses of Russia's decaying military infrastructure, these explosives are more likely than those of any other country to fall into the hands of terrorists or "rogue" states, say Western government officials and independent experts.'[30]

The Soviet security system was largely designed to protect the country's borders, prevent espionage from without and keep its people under political control; there was apparently little or no concern about domestic threats to the nuclear apparatus. With a few exceptions, such as the heavy security around the 'secret' or 'atomic' cities,[31] the physical security of materials and facilities was poor, and control and accounting procedures were rudimentary. The Soviet Union did not even have specific laws against the illicit acquisition, possession, transport and use of radioactive materials until 1988.[32] Thus, when the Soviet Union collapsed it appeared that its nuclear materials might be vulnerable to theft and misdirection, especially by impoverished and demoralised elements of the armed forces or members of the formerly privileged, but now largely redundant, nuclear workforce.

Estimates of the number of tactical nuclear weapons (TNW) possessed by the Soviet Union at the time of its dissolution vary. A Congressional Research Service paper from 1996 puts the number at 'more than 15,000';[33] another apparently authoritative report declares that the Soviet Union 'may have possessed approximately 22,000 substrategic warheads in 1991'.[34] The arsenal appears to be much smaller today. The Stockholm International Peace Research Institute (SIPRI) states that there were only 3,840 non-strategic warheads in the Russian stockpile in 2004.[35] This would appear to be a reasonably manageable number, even in less than perfect circumstances. Much of this reduction in the TNW arsenal is due to agreements on cuts between the US and the Soviet Union in 1991.

TNW have properties that are alleged to entail 'risks of early and/or unauthorized use, and ... vulnerability to theft'.[36] TNW are by definition more portable than strategic weapons. They are also designed for use by forward commanders at the battlefield level, and may therefore have fewer physical or regulatory restrictions on their arming and use. It is not obvious, however, that these characteristics necessarily make Russian TNW more vulnerable to theft than any others. In 2002, the NIC's *Annual Report to Congress on the Safety and Security of Russian Nuclear Facilities and Military Forces* said that: 'An unauthorized launch or accidental use of a Russian nuclear weapon is highly unlikely as long as current technical and procedural safeguards built into the command and control system remain in place and are effectively enforced. Our concerns about possible circumvention of the system would rise if central political authority broke down.'[37] In other words, the NIC judges the overall security of Russia's nuclear forces to be adequate, and only to be threatened by a complete failure of government. However, the report went on to say that 'the security system was designed in the Soviet era to protect weapons primarily against a threat from outside the country and may not be sufficient to meet today's challenge of a knowledgeable insider collaborating with a criminal or terrorist group'.[38]

The NIC's 2004 report also addressed the security of nuclear warheads in general:

- 'All nuclear weapons storage sites, except those subordinate to the strategic missile troops, fall under the 12th GUMO's responsibility, thus facilitating a uniform policy in matters of operation and physical security.
- In peacetime all nuclear munitions except those on ICBMs and SLBMs on alert status are stored in nuclear weapons storage sites.
- The Russians employ a multi-layered approach that includes physical, procedural, and technical measures to secure their weapons.'[39]

Globalsecurity.org describes the security around nuclear weapons under the control of the 12th GUMO in similar terms to the NIC: 'The system for the protection of nuclear munitions is echeloned and generally extremely reliable. Access to them is multilayered, and it is virtually impossible for unauthorized individual [sic] to gain access to the warheads. The transport of nuclear munitions is also properly organized. Special security units are in a high state of readiness to thwart any attempt to seize them. To date there has not been a single loss from the nuclear arsenals.'[40] Clearly, nuclear weapons are not 'strewn across Russia', nor are they 'scattered throughout' the country.

The 12th GUMO referred to above is the 12th Main Directorate of the Russian Ministry of Defence. Its direct progenitor was given charge of the Soviet Union's nuclear efforts in 1949 and the organisation, under one name or another, has held that responsibility ever since. Like the rest of the Russian armed forces, the 12th GUMO has suffered from underfunding and a decline in morale, although both seem to have improved in recent years. The 2002 NIC report quoted a 12th GUMO officer as saying in a Russian television programme in August 2001 that 'security was lax at 12th GUMO sites. The officer outlined a number of problems at the storage sites, including charges that there are personnel shortages and that alarms [sic] systems operate only 50 percent of the time. The officer speculated that a terrorist organization could seize a nuclear warhead.'[41] The report went on to discuss a number of problems affecting the 12th GUMO. These were generic to the Russian military: low, late or unpaid wages, poor housing and food shortages. While wage arrears were brought up to date by 1999 and wages have been paid regularly since then, the report quotes the 'Chief of Staff of the 12th GUMO' as saying that there were '9,500 homeless active duty and retired officers'.[42] In 1998, the head of the directorate, General-Colonel Igor Valynkin, acknowledged some 'serious incidents at some of his subordinate facilities', but added that more stringent selection criteria would be used and that polygraphs and drug and alcohol tests would 'monitor the reliability of personnel'.[43] Despite these problems, 'Valynkin was adamant that no Russian nuclear weapons had been stolen and described such allegations as "barking mad"'.[44] The 2004 NIC report does not mention any of the earlier problems with the 12th GUMO. Instead, it quotes two senior Russian officials, then First Deputy Chief of the General Staff Colonel-General Yuriy Nikolayevich Baluyevskiy and Russian Defence Minister Sergei Ivanov, as saying that Russian nuclear weapons were secure from theft by terrorists.

The greatest risk of 'leakage' was almost certainly in the months immediately following the collapse of the Soviet Union, when Russia was attempting to withdraw all nuclear weapons from the newly independent members of the old empire. Graham Allison has used courier companies such as FedEx and DHL as the standards by which to judge the likely success of these efforts. Allison argues that even professional, profit-driven companies would 'find it challenging to move so many items from so many sites in so little time without losing any'.[45] However, it is reasonable to assume that, if FedEx had been tasked with handling the most powerful weapons on earth and had been threatened with the most dire consequences if any went missing, it just might have managed a perfect success rate, especially if it had done nothing but look after nuclear weapons for the previous half century. US Vice-President Dick Cheney (then secretary of defense to President G.H.W. Bush) remarked in 1991 that a 99% success rate would constitute 'excellent' performance, though Allison points out that this would still leave '220 highly portable nuclear weapons lost, stolen, or otherwise unaccounted for'.[46] Neither Cheney nor Allison would have considered it at all excellent, however, if American troops lost a single nuclear weapon in transit, and neither, one assumes, would the Russian authorities. Nuclear weapons are not courier packages, and a level of success that might be appropriate for commercial shipping would be entirely unacceptable when applied to them.

In fact, all the evidence is that the weapons were indeed safely withdrawn. In 2002, the NIC 'assessed' that, by June 1992, 'the last of the former Soviet tactical nuclear warheads were withdrawn to Russia, and … by the end of 1996, the last of the strategic nuclear warheads had been removed from Kazakhstan, Ukraine, and Belarus'.[47] The NIC's 2004 report on Russian nuclear security quotes former Minister of Atomic Energy Yevgeny Adamov as saying: 'Neither Bin Ladin nor anyone else could steal a nuclear warhead from anywhere in the former Soviet Union. During my time as minister, I carried out a comprehensive stock-taking of everything we had and had had, and traced the history of all the warheads ever produced. So, everything there was on the territories of the former USSR republics was returned to Russia ... Nothing was stolen from us. So, neither Bin Ladin, nor Iraq nor Iran could make use of these explosive devices.'[48]

The greatest concern about 'loose' Russian nuclear weapons was triggered by General Alexander Lebed, a former chief of the Russian Security Council, who claimed in 1997 that he could account for only 48 of 100 (or 132; accounts differ) backpack-sized nuclear weapons (so-called 'suitcase nukes'). However, it is not certain that the weapons existed at all, or that, if they did, any went missing. In 2002, Nikolai Sokov, who worked on arms control at the Soviet and then Russian Ministry of Foreign Affairs between 1987 and 1992, wrote what is probably the most comprehensive review of open-source material on the topic. His paper reached two main conclusions: 'First, the probability that any portable nuclear devices were lost prior to or after the breakup of the Soviet Union appears low ... This does not mean that the threat does not exist, but rather that at this moment, it is probably not the most immediate threat to the home security of the United States or to US armed forces abroad. Second, even if any devices were lost, their effectiveness should be very low or maybe even non-existent, especially if the loss occurred during the period of the greatest risk, in the early 1990s. Without scheduled maintenance, these devices apparently can produce only minimal yield and eventually possibly no yield at all, and can only serve as a source of small amounts of weapons-grade fissile materials'.[49] Sokov described the evidence for the weapons' existence as 'sketchy and incomplete', saying they had a 'mythological quality' and 'often seem a matter of fiction rather than that of fact'. Nonetheless, he concluded that 'several broad considerations suggest that the story about portable nuclear devices should be taken seriously, with a caveat that their existence cannot be viewed as an established fact'.[50]

Even if terrorists had been able to obtain any of these weapons, Sokov argues that they would have been difficult or impossible to deploy: the bombs might have been fitted with locks to prevent unauthorised deployment, or radioactive components may have decayed to the point of uselessness. Even if it were still fresh and fully functional, terrorists would only be able to 'mine' one for its nuclear materials, which they almost certainly could not reassemble into a functional weapon. These materials could, however, be used in one or more relatively harmless RDDs. This discussion necessarily involves a good deal of speculation – state secrets are state secrets, after all, and few are more closely held than those concerning nuclear weapons – but Sokov is unusually well qualified to address the matter.

In general, at least some of the concern about loose Russian weapons may stem from an unconscious but pervasive belief that Russians cannot possibly be as responsible and effective as the Americans, the French or the British in safeguarding their nuclear arsenal, an attitude reminiscent of the demonising mythology of the Cold War, which simultaneously exaggerated the capabilities of the Soviet military, while denigrating the professionalism and competence of its members. Granted, with the near-collapse of the Russian state there was indeed a severe rise in criminality that did not exclude the armed forces, and which persists to this day. However, it is one thing to acknowledge disorder in a society simultaneously released from decades of authoritarian rule and subjected to the severe stress of economic failure; it is another altogether to allege a general abeyance of morality. Consider this excerpt from a RAND Corporation briefing paper on nuclear terrorism, which discussed the Japanese sect Aum Shinrikyo's failure to obtain nuclear weapons or technology from Russia: '*even* enterprising Russian officials and scientists *may have* feared the implications of transferring nuclear technology, knowledge, or material to a religious organization based in a foreign state … Aum's contacts may have been good, but *not good enough* to secure the transfer of such sensitive capabilities' (emphasis added).[51] The default assumptions appear to have been that 'enterprising' Russians might normally have been expected to transfer nuclear weapons or technology to an apocalyptic religious cult without considering the consequences (in other words, that they would have lacked ordinary standards of morality and responsibility); that there most likely were people in positions to do so who would indeed have handed nuclear weapons over to a cult, if only its contacts had been good enough; and that evidence to the contrary was worthy of special note, to be expressed in a tone of faint but distinct surprise.

If terrorists have indeed been seeking radioactive materials or nuclear weapons during the years since the Soviet Union's collapse, and if they are as readily available as some commentators suggest, why have terrorists – with one or two very minor exceptions – never used any radioactive materials, or shown any signs of having nuclear weapons? Similarly, why have would-be nuclear-weapon states, especially 'rogues', invested such enormous amounts of time and treasure in their quest for fissile materials, risking increasingly severe consequences, if these materials are easily available off the ex-Soviet shelf? Granted, aspirant nuclear states ideally want sustainable indigenous fuel cycles to support credible long-term deterrent or offensive capabilities, but if the aim were simply to achieve instant nuclear status, then purchasing a few Russian warheads or the fissile materials and expertise required to build an arsenal would seem to be an obvious choice. Yet to our knowledge none has taken that route, suggesting that it might not be available even to state actors, whose pockets are considerably deeper than the best-funded terrorist organisations.

The fact that there has been very little significant nuclear trafficking is no reason for complacency. Large amounts of fissile and other radioactive materials around the world are kept under less than perfect security, and will remain a proliferation threat until they are better protected. Allison points out that efforts by the remaining superpower to prevent nuclear leakage from the wreckage of the other are woefully inadequate. The US funds a number of programmes, such as the Nunn–Lugar Cooperative Threat Reduction Program, which attempt to secure nuclear weapons and materials in the former Soviet Union or to find work for underemployed ex-Soviet nuclear scientists and technicians. Yet the level of funding relative to the level of threat these programmes are meant to be addressing is dismally low – low, that is, if the American government believes what it so often says about terrorism. The Bush administration's budget for 2005 requested less than $1 billion for the Nunn–Lugar programme, and only $127 million for interdicting nuclear smuggling. The missile defence programme request, meanwhile, was for $10bn, despite the very limited potential utility of the system and the negligible threat it addresses. The invasion and occupation of Iraq has consumed immense amounts of money, despite the fact that the country never posed a credible threat to the United States. By the end of September 2005, the eventual costs of the conflict in Iraq were being put $186bn, with a further $66bn incurred in Afghanistan.[52] The comparison with the amounts spent on combating nuclear terrorism is startling. As Allison says: 'Total war on nuclear terrorism would cost $5 billion a year, or perhaps even $10 billion. In a current budget that devotes more than $500 billion to defense and the war in Iraq, a penny of every dollar for what Bush calls "our highest priority" would not be excessive.'[53]

Chapter Two

Improvised Nuclear Devices

Assuming that terrorists could collect enough fissile material, there remains the question of whether they could build a functional nuclear weapon. One school of thought says that designs for simple nuclear weapons have been in the public domain for many years, that the advent of the public Internet has only made them more accessible, and that the only significant barrier is access to materials. This view was encapsulated by the late Manhattan Project scientist Luis Alvarez, who claimed that 'terrorists, if they had such material, would have a good chance of setting off a high-yield explosion simply by dropping one half of the material onto the other half'.[1] According to the nuclear physicist Theodore Taylor, given fissile material building a bomb is 'very easy. Double underlined. Very easy.'[2] Gavin Cameron has argued that the 'design for a crude nuclear device has been publicly accessible for 25 years and relies on technology that, while challenging in the 1940s, is almost certainly no longer so'. He concludes that, if terrorists were intent on building a nuclear weapon, 'their biggest technical difficulty would probably be the acquisition of fissile material'.[3]

Others are less convinced. Another former Manhattan Project scientist, Canadian J. Carson Mark, argues that, while 'schematic drawings' for nuclear weapons have indeed been widely accessible for years, the 'detailed design drawings that are essential before it is possible to plan the fabrication of actual parts are not available'. Preparing these drawings 'requires a large number of man-hours and the direct participation of individuals thoroughly informed in several quite distinct areas: the physical, chemical and metallurgical properties of the various materials to be used, as well as the characteristics affecting their fabrication; neutronic properties; radiation effects, both nuclear and biological; technology concerning high explosives and/or chemical propellants; some hydrodynamics; electrical circuitry; and others'. In any case, 'the necessary attributes [of the nuclear weapon construction team] would be quite distinct from the paramilitary capability most often supposed to typify terrorists'.[4] Overall, Mark *et al.* support the possibility that terrorists, given enough money, time and expertise, and some very specialised equipment, not to mention sufficient quantities of fissile material, might conceivably be able to build some sort of device with a nuclear yield. Their paper is nonetheless an effective counterpoise to the notion that the procedure would be anything but difficult, time-consuming and expensive. The following discussion is based largely on their article, as it still the most authoritative technical discussion of terrorist INDs readily available.[5]

Academic Friedrich Steinhausler has set out some of the technical requirements terrorists would have to meet to build an IND. They are far from trivial, although some of the equipment listed, such as the laser interferometer, suggests that Steinhausler is discussing the construction of an implosion bomb rather than a much simpler gun-type device. According to Steinhausler, a terrorist nuclear-weapons team would need to have:

- 'basic knowledge in physical and chemical properties of fissile materials; radiation and physics; and physical principles of explosive devices, particularly about shaped charges; and electronics;
- access to a workshop with advanced equipment, such as precision calibrated, computer-guided machine tools ($\leq$ 25,000 rpm) with laser-interferometer, airbearing lathe, and artificial room ventilation with built-in air cleaner;
- acquired a sufficient amount of nuclear weapons-grade material needed for building a crude nuclear device (about 25 kg of HEU, respectively, 8 kg Pu), at least 50 kg of high explosives, and a supply of Kryton [sic] switches;
- machining capabilities for the production of complex shapes (tolerance: about 10^{-10} m); and
- ceramic (cerium sulfide) crucibles, electric furnace, argon-filled enclosure, Freon gas, and vacuum pumps'.[6]

To compound the difficulty, terrorists would probably not be able to obtain pure metallic fissile materials. The other more accessible forms of fissile material, such as powdered enriched uranium-oxide reactor fuel, uranium–plutonium ceramic MOX reactor fuel, or zirconium-clad reactor fuel elements filled with ceramic uranium-oxide pellets, would also pose significant problems. Furthermore, it is unlikely that the terrorists would know in advance exactly how much material, of what kind and isotopic composition, they would be receiving. If the nuclear black market were indeed as chaotic it appears, they might simply have to wait for nuclear material to be offered to them and then make the best of it. Building a workable device under those circumstances would be a real challenge even for a professional team; it would probably be impossible for a terrorist group. It is conceivable that terrorists could simply place an order for particular materials with a corrupt insider, although if this were a realistic possibility it would have to be asked why it appears never to have been done.

Many of the materials listed above could be used in radiation dispersal devices. However, none of them would be ideal bomb fuel, and each would require processing to make them so. Fresh reactor fuel is so poorly enriched – typically around 3–5% – that it could not be used as a nuclear explosive, and further enriching it is beyond the capacity of all but a handful of states. Used reactor fuel, unlike the fresh variety, contains some plutonium, but it is dangerously radioactive and physically hot, and extracting the plutonium 'would have to be carried out by remote operation, a very complicated undertaking requiring months to set up and check out, as well as many days for the processing itself'.[7] Extracting metallic uranium from either powdered fuel or metal fuel rods would involve some fairly difficult and potentially hazardous chemical procedures, though it 'could certainly be within the reach of a dedicated technical team'.[8]

Plutonium has bizarre physical peculiarities that can make essential steps in bomb construction – melting, casting or hot working – difficult and even potentially dangerous for the uninitiated. Metallic plutonium goes through six different crystallographic phases, more than any other element, between room temperature and its molten state, which it reaches at 640°C. As it is heated, it undergoes expansion through the alpha, beta, gamma and delta phases, but shrinks once more in the delta-prime phase, and continues to shrink, even as it heats up, until it reaches the epsilon phase, whereupon it slowly expands once more until it melts. When it does so, it abruptly shrinks once more and becomes *more* dense than the delta, delta-prime and epsilon phases, and only slightly less dense than the gamma phase.

Each phase has its own unique properties that make it more or less suitable for use in weapons. For example, the delta phase, which occurs at about 375°C, is desirable for use in weapons because it is tough and malleable, but it is not stable at room temperature. The alpha or base phase is stable and is the most dense form, but it is very brittle and the shrinkage that takes place between the liquid stage and room temperature means that it is almost impossible to accurately cast or hot-work alpha-phase plutonium. To produce a stable delta-phase metal that is easily machined or cast, plutonium has to be alloyed with a small percentage of aluminium, gallium or indium. However, plutonium does not alloy easily, so the result-ing material might have areas that were effectively pure plutonium, and therefore unstable, and others that were stable alloy. Solving this problem would almost certainly be beyond the capacity of almost any terrorist group, unless it were able to obtain some very highly specialised metallur-gical expertise. Furthermore, plutonium's liquid phase is more dense than the delta phase, which could lead to criticality problems.[9]

While neither uranium nor plutonium is particularly radioactive when fresh and unirradiated, both are chemically and radiologically toxic and carcinogenic if they enter the body,[10] and would have to be handled with some care, especially when being machined – unless, of course, members of the bomb team were willing to take the slight but real risk of developing cancer. Even if it were not carcinogenic, plutonium has other characteristics, including a tendency to burst spontaneously into flames (it is 'pyrophoric'), which mean that special care must be taken in its handling. The Rocky Flats plutonium 'pit' or weapons core production centre near Denver, Colorado, which operated from 1952 to 1989, suffered an unknown number of pluto-nium fires, including at least three particularly serious incidents. The local fire brigade responded to 31 plutonium fires between 1966 and 1969 alone. However, the actual number of plutonium fires at Rocky Flats may never be accurately known.[11] When plutonium filings or chips ignited spontane-ously, workers dropped them into machine oil to put them out.[12] Clearly, there are hazards other than radiation or criticality awaiting the unwary or careless bomb builder, especially if they want to use plutonium.

According to Mark et al., using very highly enriched uranium-oxide powder (94% U-235) or reactor-grade plutonium oxide powder as-is would probably be 'the simplest and most rapid way to make a bomb' because of the difficulty involved in converting it into metallic form.[13] In this case, terrorists would need very large quantities of fuel. The bare critical mass ('bare crit') for powdered HEU oxide at full crystal density – which is very much denser than the form in which it would most probably be obtained – is about 110kg (242lb), and about 35kg (77lb) for plutonium oxide.[14] Using an implosion design with neutron reflectors, such as plates of iron, natural uranium or graphite, would reduce the amount required by half, but this would also substantially increase the device's weight and bulk.[15] Amory Lovins claims that 'neutron reflection and implosion can reduce critical mass by a large factor. This factor has been officially stated to be ~5, consistent with the US and IAEA requirement of strict physical security measures for quantities of Pu≥2 kg (independent of isotopic composition). Published data suggest, however, that with sophisticated design the factor may be > 5.'[16] The most effective neutron reflector, one that could achieve the kinds of economies suggested by Lovins, is beryllium.

Lower enrichment grades of uranium could theoretically be used in weapons, although the amounts required would be immense: the bare crit for 50%-enriched uranium is about 160kg (350lb); for 20%-enriched uranium, the lowest grade still considered highly enriched, it would be 800kg (1760lb).[17] If sufficient amounts of powder were obtained, 'the terrorists would [still] need accurate information in advance concerning the physical state, isotopic composition and chemical constituents' of the material, and would also require a larger quantity of material and 'a larger weight in the assembly mechanism to bring the material into an explosive configuration' than would be required for metallic bomb fuels: 'Even [if the powder were] at full crystal density, the amounts are large enough to appear troublesome: ~55kg (half bare crit) for 94 percent uranium oxide and ~17.5kg for plutonium. However, the density of powder as acquired is nowhere close to crystal density. To approach crystal density would require a large and special press, and the attempt to acquire [one] … might blow the cover of a clandestine operation … The option of using low-density powder in a gun-type assembly should probably be excluded on the basis of the large material requirements. There remains the possibility of using a rather large amount of oxide powder (tens of kilograms or possibly more) at low density in an implosion-type assembly and simply counting on the applied pressure to increase the density sufficiently to achieve a nuclear explosion. Some sort of workable device could certainly be achieved in that way. However, obtaining a persuasive determination of the actual densities that would be realised in a porous material under shock pressure (and thence the precise amount of material required) would be a very difficult theoretical (and experimental) problem for a terrorist team.'[18]

The need for fast conventional high explosives (HE) imposes an entirely different set of technical and safety considerations. All nuclear weapons, whether gun or implosion types, require high assembly velocities because of the risk of pre-initiation or 'fizzle' due to neutron sources in the fuel that could trigger a chain reaction before the fissile material was properly assembled into a supercritical configuration. If that happened, the weapon could simply be blown apart, with minimal nuclear yield.[19] If assembly velocities were reasonably high, however, the 'fizzle yield' of a crude device could be in the 100-tonne HE equivalent range. The risk of predetonation is so high for plutonium of any grade that it cannot be used in a gun-type assembly.

A military gun-type device assembles its components in approximately one millisecond; compression of the fissile core in an implosion device takes one to four *microseconds*.[20] Terrorists, however, are likely to require even higher assembly velocities in their weapons because of the characteristics of the fuel they would be likely to use.[21] In practical terms, this means that, in order to prevent fizzle caused by the neutron source, a terrorist gun-type uranium bomb would require both a longer barrel than a military weapon, to allow the projectile to accelerate before hitting the target, and more, or more powerful, explosives to drive the projectile, both of which would considerably increase the bomb's weight and bulk over a military weapon, as would the sheer mass of the fissile powder and associated materials. Similarly, the strong neutron source in reactor-grade plutonium means that a bomb made from this material would require exceedingly high implosion velocities.

Building an implosion bomb – the only kind that can be made with plutonium – is a significantly more difficult technical challenge than a gun device because of the need to generate a powerful, perfectly spherical shockwave that converges on the fuel core, typically a solid or hollow metal sphere or 'pit', compressing it over the course of two to three microseconds into a supercritical configuration two or more times as dense as the original metal. This requires an assembly of HE shaped charges, or explosive 'lenses', arranged in a sphere around the pit, which must be triggered with extreme speed and accuracy. If the lenses do not go off simultaneously, or as close to simultaneously as technically possible, the shockwaves would not converge at the centre, the pit would be distorted and not properly compressed and the nuclear yield could be compromised, if there was any yield at all. To build this kind of weapon, terrorists would need advanced knowledge of high explosives, metallurgy and hydrodynamics, as well as some highly restricted items, such as krytrons or similar ultra-high speed switches, sometimes called nuclear triggers,[22] in addition to their skills in nuclear physics. Nevertheless, the US Department of Defense claims that the 'technical problems confronting the designer of an implosion-assembled improvised nuclear device (IND) are relatively simple in comparison to obtaining special nuclear materials, particularly if the IND does not have to be very safe or predictable in yield'.[23]

The technical challenges involved in building a nuclear weapon are severe, although not – in theory at least – utterly insuperable, given enough time, money, materials, knowledge and equipment. In Mark *et al.*'s view: 'several conclusions concerning crude devices based on early design principles can be made. 1. Such a device could be constructed by a group not previously engaged in designing or building nuclear weapons, providing a number of requirements were adequately met. 2. Successful execution would require the efforts of a team having knowledge and skills additional to those usually associated with a group engaged in hijacking a transport or conducting a raid on a plant. 3. To achieve rapid turnaround (that is, the device would be ready within a day or so after obtaining the material), careful preparations extending over a considerable period would have to have been carried out, and the materials acquired would have to be in the form prepared for. 4. The amounts of fissile material necessary would tend to be large – certainly several, and possibly ten times, the so-called formula quantities. 5. The weight of the complete device would also be large – not as large as the first atomic weapons (~10,000 pounds), since these required aero dynamic cases to enable them to be handled as bombs, but probably more than a ton.'[24]

Amateur and 'low end' weapon design
The Nth Country Experiment

There are some examples in the literature of attempts by 'amateurs' – the term is used loosely – to design nuclear weapons without specialised knowledge of the field. One of the better known, although it is still largely classified, is the 'Nth Country Experiment', carried out by the United States in the mid-1960s. The experiment took place 'at a time when policymakers wanted to know how difficult it would be for a non-nuclear power to develop a nuclear weapons capability. The stated purpose was to "see if a few capable physicists, unfamiliar with nuclear weapons and with access only to the unclassified technology, could produce a credible weapon design".'[25]

The team members chosen for the experiment were not experienced weapon designers, nor did they have access to classified material. They were not, however, unprepared for their task. The two original members, David A. Dobson and David N. Pipkorn, were described in the *Bulletin of the Atomic Scientists*, which interviewed Dobson and others involved in the project nearly 40 years later, as post-doctoral physicists.[26] Each would have had about nine years of advanced education in physics and mathematics, as well as exposure to other branches of the natural sciences and technology.

Dobson was a published nuclear physicist[27] by the time the experiment got under way in May 1964, while Pipkorn published a paper[28] on the physics of iron under extreme pressure not long thereafter. Both fields are clearly of more than passing relevance to weapon design. When they were recruited, both were working at the Lawrence Radiation Laboratory (LRL), later part of the Lawrence Livermore National Laboratory (LLNL). When Pipkorn left the project in its second year, he was replaced by Robert W. Selden, an LRL Army Research Associate with a doctorate in physics.

The declassified version of the report on the experiment is heavily censored and abridged. Only 15 of at least 55 pages of a summary report are available, and on some pages only a few words are visible.[29] Luckily, Dobson, Selden and others have been more expansive in later interviews. One particularly interesting, and possibly rather ominous, feature of the project was that the team chose to design an implosion weapon using plutonium, rather than a gun-style bomb, on the grounds that the latter was too easy and designing one would have been, as Dobson put it, 'a pretty crummy showing'. The implosion method, on the other hand, 'seemed to be a more sophisticated, challenging, and hence appealing problem'.[30] According to Dobson, the team designed detonators, explosive lenses, the uranium tamper, the plutonium core and a polonium–beryllium initiator 'inspired by the standard neutron source used to start reactors'.[31] They concluded the project in 1965 with a set of blueprints for machinists: 'Their weapon was too big to fit on a missile, but small enough to be carried by an aircraft or truck. More interested in guaranteeing an explosion than in maximizing yield, they went with a conservative design. ("We weren't trying to get fancy and optimize things", said Dobson.) The same philosophy guided the first nuclear explosives of the United States, Britain, Russia and China, all of which came in at around 20 kilotons.'[32]

The experiment also pointed to some of the risks involved in bomb design and construction by true amateurs: 'In a less theoretical situation, "preliminary experimentation" might prove deadly to would-be bomb makers. Hudgins [Physicist Art Hudgins], who oversaw the experiment, knew that from reviewing some of the amateur bomb designs that came in "over the transom" to the federal government. "Usually they used too much uranium, plutonium", he said. "They had not given proper attention to what would happen when they assembled their bomb, or even when they were just working with the uranium and plutonium. People just figure they'll use lots of uranium and then they'll have enough".'[33]

Nonetheless, Dobson believed that terrorists might be able to build a nuclear weapon: 'It seems to me that this Al Qaeda is enough of an organization, with enough people and enough funding that they probably could.'[34] Selden agreed: 'That's the key question of the time we live in, whether or not that can be done … It's certainly possible for a terrorist group if they're really technically savvy and have a lot of resources.'[35] However, Selden has also highlighted the difficulties involved in designing and fuelling a weapon: 'Obtaining the fissile material is really the major problem – that drives the whole project … But the process of designing the weapon – I'm always careful to point out that many people overstate how easy it is. You really have to do it right, and there are thousands of ways to do it wrong. You can't just guess.'[36]

The teenager's 10kt beachball

In 1977 an undergraduate at Princeton University, John Aristotle Phillips, attempted to develop a working design for a nuclear weapon for his senior thesis. According to Graham Allison, Phillips based his work on freely available publications, such as *The Los Alamos Primer: The First Lectures on How to Build an Atomic Bomb* by Robert Serber.[37] Phillips allegedly succeeded in designing 'a perfect terrorist weapon: a bomb the size of a beach ball, with a 10 kiloton yield and a price tag of $2,000'.[38]

This is an extraordinary claim. Miniaturising nuclear weapons is one of the most difficult problems facing military designers, and yet Allison suggests that an undergraduate student with no specialist training was able not only to design a bomb, but a miniature one to boot, in just five months. The physics package alone of the Fat Man bomb dropped on Nagasaki was approximately basketball-sized. The fully functional bomb was aptly named: at 3.13m long and 147cm in diameter, and weighing 4,682kg, it was rather larger than a basketball. Granted, those dimensions included an aerodynamic housing and fins, and the bomb had a larger yield (25 kilotons), but it is still difficult to imagine how an undergraduate could have achieved such an astonishing reduction in scale, especially since he was concerned with designing 'a Crude Pu^{239} Fission Bomb'.[39]

The smallest nuclear weapon known to have been built by the United States was the minuscule W-54 warhead used in the *Davy Crockett* recoilless rifle projectile, the B-54 or M129/M159 Small Atomic Demolition Munition (SADM) and the GAR-11/AIM-26A *Falcon* air-to-air missile. It was a high-efficiency plutonium implosion device, measuring about 26.4cm by 38.5cm and weighing around 22.8kg. Its yield was proportionately tiny: between 0.01kt and 0.25kt. Even the most powerful member of the W-54 family was about 40 times less powerful than the device allegedly designed by Phillips. The US arsenal has included relatively small warheads with immense 'pow

Jim Sanborn, 'Laboratory Environment for the Assembly of the Trinity Device'. The components of the physics package are displayed on the tables at a safe distance from one another in this artist's mock-up of a Manhattan Project laboratory at Los Alamos. Image courtesy of the artist and the Numark Gallery, Washington DC.

per pound', such as the 44cm by 113cm W-47 thermonuclear warhead, which yielded up to 1.2Mt.[40] Other physically small warheads, such as the members of the MK/B-61 family, yielded as much as 340kt, but these were also true thermonuclear devices – a far cry indeed from the 'crude' fission design allegedly developed by Phillips.[41] One can only conclude that either Allison reported the design's supposed yield incorrectly, or that Phillips was mistaken about its likely yield.

An artistic representation of Fat Man

One of the most intriguing recent examples of amateur design was by an American artist, Jim Sanborn, who built an art installation using a number of pieces of equipment from the original Los Alamos laboratory of the Manhattan Project. This contained what has been described as a remarkably accurate rendition of the physics package, comprising the fissile fuel as well as other parts, of the *Trinity* test device ('the Gadget'). The same design was used in the Fat Man bomb. It was based on 'what is now widely recognized as the best estimates ever made about … the main components of the "gadget" before it was wrapped in high explosives and inserted in the bomb ... Proceeding outwards from the center are: the initiator (or urchin), about one inch in diameter; the plutonium pit, 3.62 inches; the uranium tamper, nine inches; the thickness of the boron-plastic shell, about three-sixteenths of an inch; and the aluminum pusher shell, 18 inches.'[42]

Sanborn based his models on calculations made by an amateur historian and truck driver, John Coster-Mullen, which took as their departure point a photograph of a box containing the *Trinity* physics package being loaded into a car.[43] Coster-Mullen apparently has no formal scientific training beyond high school. Nonetheless, Robert S. Norris, a senior researcher at the Natural Resources Defense Council, said of the installation that 'none of the original labs at Los Alamos remain. This is the closest we are going to get to what it was really like.' He went on to say that Coster-Mullen's research was a 'unique contribution ... It was all out there for someone to find and he did it.'[44]

South Africa: 'quick and dirty' bombs?
South Africa occupies a unique position in being the only country with a nuclear-weapons capability to willingly turn itself into a country without this capability and accede to the Nuclear Non-Proliferation Treaty (NPT), which it did on 10 July 1991.[45]

The South African nuclear-weapon programme produced six very basic gun-type bombs. It is often suggested that this programme is a kind of paradigm case for terrorist proliferation, in that the country chose the cheapest and most direct – or quickest and dirtiest – route to nuclear-weapon status. The US Department of Defense has characterised South Africa's programme as having been at an 'intermediate' level, between the 'low end', at which 'a nation may find a way to obtain a complete working nuclear bomb from a willing or unwilling supplier', and 'the other end', at which a country establishes a 'complete nuclear infrastructure' with the capacity to design and build true thermonuclear weapons using domestically sourced materials. In other words, South Africa was at the same point that terrorist proliferators might be expected to occupy.

The South African programme is said to have involved a 'total project cost of less than $1 billion (1980's purchasing power)' and used 'no more than 400 people and indigenous technology'.[46] While these figures are relatively small on the scale of national nuclear-weapons programmes, they are far beyond the capacities of any known terrorist group. Despite the fact that the majority of its population has long been mired in poverty and illiteracy, South Africa was – and remains – the wealthiest country in Africa, able to support world-class development in various technical and scientific areas, albeit on a small scale. It provided high levels of education for a small white élite, either at domestic institutions or by sending students to train overseas. Finally, until the mid-1970s and the start of meaningful international reaction against the apartheid regime, it enjoyed full membership of the international community, with the usual technological and scientific exchanges that take place between friendly states. Some of those exchanges involved nuclear technology: 'In the 1950s and 1960s, South Africa's civilian nuclear program received extensive assistance from abroad. Staff members were sent to Europe and the United States for training in various nuclear fields. South Africa was able to build a solid nuclear infrastructure. This foundation was undoubtedly important in its efforts to obtain nuclear weapons. During this period, the United States supplied South Africa with the Safari-1 research reactor, which was commissioned in 1965 at the Pelindaba Nuclear Research Center and subjected to IAEA safeguards. Over the next 10 years, the United States supplied the reactor with about 100 kilograms of weapon-grade uranium fuel.'[47]

South Africa has the world's fourth-largest uranium reserves[48] and has been a significant producer for many years. In the early 1960s, it began a secret programme to develop an indigenous system for enriching uranium. A unique stationary wall vortex tube technique, using similar basic principles to those employed by the more common and more efficient gas centrifuge design, was proven in 1969, and publicly announced in 1970. A full-scale plant began full operation in 1977. The uranium-enrichment programme was never exclusively military; it also produced 3.25% LEU fuel elements for the country's French-supplied pressurised water reactor (PWR) power plant (the only one in Africa), at Koeberg near Cape Town, and 45% HEU fuel for the SAFARI-1 reactor after American fuel supplies were cut off in 1976.

In the 1960s, more-or-less in parallel with American efforts in the same direction, South Africa began a 'very modest investigation, confined to literature studies' into the peaceful use of nuclear explosives.[49] In 1971, with the prospect of a steady supply of indigenously produced HEU, the Atomic Energy Bureau conducted a feasibility study into producing peaceful nuclear explosives (PNEs). The study led to approval of 'a programme for the development of a nuclear explosive capability for peaceful applications which also included the development of a testing site for an underground test'.[50] The programme's official goals remained peaceful until 1977, when South Africa began to develop a strategic nuclear deterrent capability. The first full-scale gun-type device was completed by the Atomic Energy Corporation (AEC) in the same year. It was intended for a fully instrumented test using depleted uranium (DU) at an underground test site in the Kalahari desert, but the test was never carried out. A second, smaller device was built in 1978, and fuelled in November 1979 with indigenously produced 80% HEU. The state arms corporation ARMSCOR took over the designing and building of nuclear explosives from the AEC in 1979, and by 1981 a new dedicated production facility outside Pretoria had been commissioned. It produced its first bomb in December 1982. In all, six devices were made.

The South African bombs were of simple design. In particular, they lacked neutron initiators, which are used in virtually all other designs to start the explosive fission chain reaction. Modern initiators are essentially miniature linear particle accelerators, often also referred to as pulse neutron tubes or neutron generators, that reside outside the weapon's core. Initiators are not easy to make: 'Few nations other than the five nuclear weapons states have mastered the techniques of constructing initiators. Presumably the three nuclear threshold states [North Korea, Pakistan and Israel] have; Iraq made substantial progress, and South Africa elected not to use an initiator.'[51] The bombs apparently used only natural background radiation to initiate the reaction, although it is not clear exactly how this was done, nor whether the choice significantly affected the scientific and engineering effort. Terrorist weapon designers would probably also perforce opt not to use initiators.

Despite the simplicity of its weapons, the South African programme was intended to provide safe and reliable weapons for a state arsenal, and it is often correctly pointed out that the standards that would apply under those circumstances would not apply to terrorists: 'Acquisition of a militarily significant nuclear capability involves, however, more than simply the purchase or construction of a single nuclear device or weapon. It requires attention to issues of safety and handling of the weapons, reliability and predictability of entire systems, efficient use of scarce and valuable special nuclear material (SNM) (plutonium and enriched uranium), chains of custody and procedures for authorizing the use of the weapons, and the careful training of the military personnel who will deliver weapons to their targets. In contrast, a nuclear device used for terrorism need not be constructed to survive a complex stockpile-to-target sequence, need not have a predictable and reliable yield, and need not be efficient in its use of nuclear material.'[52]

Some of these conditions would not have applied to the South African programme: it was never intended to support long-term, open-ended production, and the South African army was already highly trained and battle-tested. Some of these conditions also might not apply to terrorists: in particular, they might have to be excessively careful in their use of fissile materials. Given the tiny amounts that are known to have been smuggled, they would probably struggle to assemble even the smallest critical mass. The crucial point about the South African programme is that it took at least three years, from 1974 to 1977, for a relatively wealthy state with an existing nuclear infrastructure, years of friendly international exchange of nuclear technology and knowledge and high levels of domestic expertise to build a simple gun-type device that could have produced a nuclear yield.[53] States do indeed have higher standards than terrorists, but these would be more than offset by the very much lower levels of funding, expertise, staffing and equipment available to terrorists. And that ignores the major problem facing terrorists: obtaining a sufficient supply of fissile materials of known composition. If South Africa is indeed a model for terrorist proliferation, there is probably little need to worry.

An unholy bomb?: the Aum Shinrikyo

The Japanese Aum Shinrikyo cult is best known for its sarin nerve-gas attack on the Tokyo metro system in 1995.[54] It is less widely known, however, that the cult resorted to chemical and biological weapons only after it had invested a good deal of money and effort in an unsuccessful attempt to become history's first non-state nuclear power. The cult's attempts to develop a nuclear capability crudely approximated those of a state, at least at the outset. It appears to have wanted to develop a complete 'indigenous' weapons capability, from mining and enriching uranium to building bombs, although it went about it in a haphazard fashion.

The nuclear project began in earnest in 1993, when the cult bought a number of mining leases on an Australian sheep ranch with a known uranium deposit. It also explored the feasibility of buying a ship to move uranium ore overseas. Earthmoving and rock-crushing equipment was brought to the ranch, and a small laboratory was set up. Although its activities during its short tenure on the ranch remain mysterious, Aum is known to have tested sarin gas on some of the sheep there. Also in 1993, the group tried to buy a sophisticated laser measuring device (an interferometer), designated as 'dual-use' by the US government because it can measure, with great precision, the velocity of high explosives or the surface of a uranium or plutonium sphere for use in a nuclear weapon. Aum also attempted to buy a vibration isolation table that could be used for the same purpose. However, the manufacturer became suspicious and alerted the

US export authorities, and neither sale was completed. The cult also tried to buy a $450,000 laser welder from a Californian company, indicating that the machine was to be used in a sealed room and operated via a glove box, which would only have been necessary in the presence of hazardous materials, including radioactive substances. When 'a member of the cult's Science and Technology Agency' was arrested in March 1995, he was carrying a document about laser enrichment.[55]

As Cameron points out, Aum's interest in this technology is puzzling. Laser isotope separation is a complex, difficult and technology intensive operation compared with other established methods, such as gas centrifuge, gaseous diffusion or electromagnetic ion separation (also known as the Calutron method). 'It is very difficult to master and is not the obvious first step for a proliferator.'[56] Cameron goes on to say, with a nice degree of understatement, that 'Aum's attempts to construct a nuclear-yield weapon were somewhat idiosyncratic'.[57] Some of their activities suggest that the cultists were interested in an implosion bomb, probably because of its fuel efficiency, but they are not known to have investigated some basic elements of that design, such as neutron reflectors and shaped charges, and their interest in laser enrichment seems to have been an expression of their leader's fascination with lasers, rather than the product of rational engineering.

Aum's parallel efforts to obtain nuclear technologies, materials or bombs from the former Soviet Union began when the cult's leader Shoko Asahara met a number of senior Russian politicians and scientists, including Vice-President Aleksandr Rutskoi, the speaker of the Russian Parliament Ruslan Khasbulatov, the secretary of Russia's Security Council, Oleg Lobov, and Nikolai Basov, who won the Nobel prize for physics in 1962 for his work on lasers.[58] Lobov and Asahara became friends, and Lobov gave Aum an old building in Moscow; Aum, meanwhile, gave Lobov between $500,000 and $1m between 1991 and 1995 'for reasons that have never been explained'.[59] Asahara is said to have bribed or attempted to bribe a number of senior Russian officials in an attempt to obtain 'sensitive military technologies', while the Russian intelligence services may have helped Aum to acquire military technologies in a bid to gain access to secrets that the cult had stolen from Japanese research establishments.[60] The cult recruited thousands of members in Russia, including staff from the Kurchatov Institute in Moscow, a leading nuclear research centre holding hundreds of kilograms of weapons-usable HEU, and physicists from Moscow State University. Aum even sought a meeting with Minister of Atomic Energy Victor Mikhailov in an attempt to purchase a nuclear weapon.[61] Most of the Russians mentioned denied meeting Aum members, but a RAND corporation report says that 'US Senate investigators found photos in Aum publications that showed Rutskoy, Khasbulatov, Basov, and Lobov with Asahara'.[62]

Kiyohide Hayakawa, Aum's 'minister of construction' (Aum structured itself as an alternative government of Japan), made eight trips to Russia in 1994. His personal notebook contained a 'shopping list' including a nuclear warhead, for which Aum was prepared to pay $15m. While he did not buy a nuclear weapon, Hayakawa may have obtained a recipe for sarin from Russia, possibly from Lobov himself. The sarin Aum used in Tokyo followed a formula unique to the Russian military, and Aum's head of intelligence, Yoshihiro Inoue, claimed at his 1997 trial that Lobov was its source. Hayakawa's notebook also contained detailed notes on the production of sarin.[63] Despite its 30,000 Russian members, its $1bn war chest, its scientists, its attempts to recruit post-Soviet expertise and its high-level political contacts, Aum was never able to acquire a nuclear weapon or nuclear technology from Russia, even in the chaotic years shortly after the Soviet Union's collapse. While this does not prove that Russian nuclear weapons are not 'loose', it is persuasive evidence that they have been more tightly controlled than some believe, even soon after the collapse of the Soviet Union.

CHAPTER THREE

Terrorist Psychology, Motivation and Strategy

Discussion about the terrorist use of WMD typically begins, and usually ends, with essentially technical questions. Can terrorists obtain the necessary materials? Do they have the skills to make weapons out of them? Can they deploy them? The underlying assumption often appears to be that any and all terrorists want WMD and, given the opportunity, would happily use them.

Some of the problems of this approach should already be obvious. First, 'terrorists' are far from constituting a homogeneous group, despite the misleading way terrorism is currently treated,[1] as though it were somehow a single distinguishable entity, rather than a tactic that a wide range of actors, including individuals, subnational or transnational groups and states, may employ. Terrorists vary considerably in their political aims, their strategic and geopolitical situations, their technical capabilities and their psychological and strategic motivations.

Second, there is a tendency in political and popular discourse to lump all WMD together. Again, while they all have the theoretical ability to cause mass casualties, these weapons differ greatly in almost every other respect. Creating an indigenous nuclear-weapon capability requires state-level resources invested over many years, and building a functional nuclear weapon may well be beyond the abilities of any known terrorist group. On the other hand, radiological weapons can be very easy to build, depending on their type, and radioactive materials could be obtained relatively easily, but no radiological weapon would have anything like the destructive power or lethality of a true fission device. Likewise, biological, biotoxic and chemical WMD all have a unique set of characteristics that would affect their value for any given strategy or group. Like terrorists, WMD are not interchangeable. This chapter concentrates on nuclear, and to a lesser extent radiological, weapons. It attempts to assess the likelihood that any non-state subnational or transnational group might 'go nuclear'.

Terrorist psychologies

Popular and political rhetoric is full of descriptions of terrorists as 'sick', 'crazy', 'psychopathic', or even 'psychotic'.[2] This is a dangerously misleading notion that can seriously undermine our attempts to understand terrorist behaviour. Terrorist activity cannot be dismissed as 'irrational' and hence as pathological, unreasonable or inexplicable. The resort to terrorism need not be an aberration; it may be a reasonable and calculated response to circumstances.[3] Most terrorists are psychologically normal and as rational as most other people: 'Whilst many [terrorists] are violent, and most have committed horrific and sometimes barbaric crimes, few if any fit the image in any technical sense of an abnormal individual … Most active terrorists show few if any of the attributes of clinical abnormality. In a statistical sense, terrorists are not "normal", by virtue of the lives they lead and the things they do. But there seems [sic] to be no discernible psychopathological qualities of terrorists that can identify them in any clinical sense as different from others in the community from which they come.'[4] That terrorists do things that are abhorrent or incomprehensible to others says more about ordinary people than most of us are willing to admit, despite the overwhelming historical evidence that extreme violence, in the form of wars, genocide, murder and rape, is part of the common human heritage.

Jerrold M. Post, the founder of the CIA's Center for the Analysis of Personality and Political Behavior (CAPPB), agrees: 'The author's own comparative research on the psychology of terrorists does not reveal major psychopathology, and is in substantial agreement with the findings of Crenshaw that "the outstanding common characteristic of terrorists is their normality". Her studies of the National Liberation Front (FLN) in Nigeria in the 1950s found the members to be basically normal. Nor did Heskin find members of the Irish Republican Army (IRA) to be emotionally disturbed.' In a review of the social psychology of terrorist groups, McCauley and Segal conclude that the best documented generalization is negative; terrorists do not show any striking psychopathology. Nor does a comparative study reveal a 'particular psychological type, a particular personality constellation, a uniform terrorist mind'.[5]

Seriously disturbed people, especially those suffering from psychosis, usually have great difficulty in doing day-to-day tasks, like keeping a job, maintaining a household or staying healthy. Engaging in the demanding clandestine activities required by terrorism would simply be beyond the capabilities of a psychotic person. Moreover, people with serious mental illness could constitute a grave danger to 'professional' terrorist organisations, in the extremely unlikely event that they were recruited in the first place. Indeed, they are unlikely to be anything but an impediment and a security risk to any terrorist organisation. Even people with less serious disorders, such as depression or bipolar disorder, could be lethargic and unmotivated, or intermittently unpredictable and potentially uncontrollable. Personality disorders could affect the sufferer's sense of loyalty or their reliability. In short, all of the factors that can make mental illness so disabling in the workplace and in daily life would also be at play in terrorist organisations, a situation further complicated by the need for strict discipline, secrecy and the ability to preserve a façade of normality while leading a double life.

It is sometimes suggested that one personality type – the antisocial personality, formerly known as the psychopath – is particularly suited to violent terrorism. It is true that many, but not all, people with antisocial personality disorder can be violent, sometimes extremely so. It is also true, almost by definition, that people with the full-blown disorder have no conscience and feel no remorse for their actions. However, 'psychopaths' also have characteristics that could make them unsuitable for most terrorist organisations. They are selfish and deeply resistant to external discipline; to the extent that they follow orders, they do so only under duress or for as long as they perceive doing so to be in their immediate interests. Finally, they can be highly impulsive. All of these traits make antisocial personalities risky partners in any sort of enterprise, especially one that requires secrecy, rigid discipline, long-term planning, the ability to cooperate with others and the will and ability to endure privation and stress in the service of a cause, with little or no prospect of personal reward. However, people with less extreme forms of antisocial personality disorder – marked antisocial traits, in clinical terms – could be functional in terrorist groups. The violence and excitement would appeal, while their indifference to the feelings of others could make them valuable as 'soldiers', the operatives who actually carry out terrorist actions.

Although most serious forms of psychopathology would disqualify their sufferers from working as terrorists, it is clear that some, especially terrorist leaders, have shown traits characteristic of personality disorders;

there can, for instance, be little doubt that the leaders of a number of groups have shown signs of narcissistic personality disorder: 'The symptoms of narcissistic personality disorder revolve around a pattern of grandiosity, need for admiration and sense of entitlement. Often, individuals feel overly important and will exaggerate achievements and will accept, and often demand, praise and admiration ... There is a sense of entitlement, of being more deserving than others based solely on their superiority.'[6] Shoko Asahara, the former leader of Aum Shinrikyo, is a good example. He had numerous titles, including 'yogi', 'venerated master' and 'holy pope', and claimed to be the reincarnated Jesus Christ and the first 'enlightened one' since the Buddha.[7] Asahara also had paranoid traits, with clear delusions of persecution.[8]

Osama bin Laden has been alleged to have a personality disorder, or at least to show personality traits exaggerated to a pathological degree. Post has called him a 'malignant narcissist' who 'thrives on being on center stage and wants to influence world events ... Part of what he's been trying to do [by releasing statements and videos] is to keep up this tension, which magnifies his stature and accomplishes many of his goals.'[9] Bruce Hoffman of the RAND Corporation concurs: 'bin Laden has a certain sense of vanity and hubris in his mindset. He feels he has single-handedly changed the course of history, and to a certain extent, it's true. There's not many people who can say that.'[10] Based on the limited information provided by his public statements and actions, bin Laden does not appear to want or encourage a personality cult, and his public speeches and writings are phrased in terms of a *jihad* by or on behalf of the greater Muslim community against infidel aggressors and corrupt Arab governments, rather than in terms of himself as a particularly special, blessed or gifted person. He does, however, require members of al-Qaeda and its affiliates to swear *bay'ah*, or personal loyalty, to him. He also eschewed a life of considerable wealth and ease to live in hiding, under constant stress and deprivation, in the service of his beliefs. This is not to say that asceticism and malignant narcissism are necessarily incompatible, but asceticism in itself surely does not support the diagnosis. If bin Laden is indeed narcissistic, his narcissism is of a quite different order than Asahara's. This is by no means to support or condone bin Laden, his beliefs or his actions in any way. The point is simply that, in order to deal appropriately with terrorists, it is necessary to understand them as they are, not as the demonised stereotypes that popular and political discourse apparently require. That terrorists may be, and in fact frequently are, intelligent, psychologically healthy idealists only makes them more dangerous, not less.

Post has argued that terrorist violence itself, rather than the cause for which it is ostensibly employed, is or rapidly becomes the group's *raison d'être*. Post bases his claim on the belief that, while they do not show any particular psychopathology, many terrorists are aggressive, stimulus-seeking, excitement-hungry, but socially and economically insignificant men with marked feelings of inadequacy: '[I do not] view political violence as instrumental, but as the end itself. *The cause is not the cause.* The cause, as codified in the group's ideology, according to this line of reasoning, becomes the rationale for the acts the terrorists are driven to commit. Indeed, the central argument of this position is that *individuals become terrorists in order to join terrorist groups and commit acts of terrorism'* (emphases in original).[11] Post also argues that success in terms of the terrorist group's stated goals would remove its reason for being: 'For any group or organization, the highest priority is survival. This is especially true for the terrorist group. To succeed in achieving its espoused cause would threaten the goal of survival. This fact suggests a position of cybernetic balance for the group. It must be successful enough in its terrorist acts and rhetoric of legitimation to attract members and perpetuate itself, but it must not be so successful that it will succeed itself out of business.'[12]

While it is obviously, and trivially, true that there are psychological roots to all human behaviour, to reduce all behaviour to psychology in this limited sense usually results in reductions *ad absurdum.* In other words, if one were to consistently apply Post's arguments, almost any group or institution could be seen as existing merely to serve its members' psychological needs, with its overt function taking a somewhat distant second place. If the highest priority for any group is survival and the service of its members' psyches, how are we to explain the many examples of groups that have cheerfully dissolved themselves when their goals were accomplished? The worldwide multitude of passionate and highly organised anti-apartheid groups did not all suddenly invoke new causes to sustain their existences when, partly because of their efforts, South Africa became a democracy in 1994. Terrorism and other forms of political violence arise in response to objective social, cultural, political and economic conditions, and have more-or-less explicit political goals. Groups such as Hamas, al-Qaeda or the Irish Republican Army (IRA) are not social clubs that exist solely to provide an outlet for their members' aggressive drives.

Motivations and constraints

If terrorists are not irrational psychotic or psychopathic killers, it must be accepted that they are rational actors – or at least as rational as the rest of us – with goals and even ideals, who devise and execute strategies, who calculate costs and benefits and who are responsive to internal and external incentives and constraints, whether psychological, social, cultural, political, financial or technical. The costs could be very high. Martha Crenshaw argues that, not only does terrorism 'invariably invite a punitive government reaction' by causing civilian deaths, but it can also alienate potential supporters, both domestic and international.[13] However, Crenshaw also notes that terrorism has an 'extremely useful agenda setting function': 'If the reasons behind violence are skillfully articulated, terrorism can put the issue of political change on the public agenda. By attracting attention it makes the claims of the resistance a salient issue in the public mind. The government can reject but not ignore an opposition's demands.'[14] In general, Crenshaw says that 'The reasoning behind terrorism takes into account the balance of power between challengers and authorities, a balance that depends on the amount of popular support the resistance can mobilize. The proponents of terrorism understand this constraint and possess reasonable expectations about the likely results of action or inaction. They may be wrong about the alternatives that are open to them, or miscalculate the consequences of their actions, but their decisions are based on logical processes.'[15]

Any terrorist group contemplating mass-casualty or mass-destruction terrorism, especially nuclear terrorism, does so within the context of a number of constraining or facilitating factors. Politically and strategically, these include the group's internal dynamics and leadership, its claimed or actual constituency, its relationship with its host state or states, the latter's and their own susceptibility to deterrence, their positions in the international system, the terrorists' target or targets and the likely lethality or destructiveness of the contemplated attack. There are also psychosocial factors that might differentiate between groups that are otherwise similarly situated. In many ways, nuclear terrorism is a special case of mass-casualty, mass-destruction, terrorism: while it is not at all clear for technical reasons that terrorist RDDs, in particular, would in fact cause either mass casualties or mass destruction, the decision to 'go nuclear' would necessarily involve the intention to do so. In other words, the psychological step from deciding to engage in mass-casualty terror to going nuclear is a much smaller one than that involved in deciding to engage in mass-casualty terror in the first place.

This discussion focuses on the motivation – the strategic calculations and psychosocial capacity – involved in going nuclear, regardless of the technical ability to do so. It follows Post's typology, with some amendments. It lists nationalist-separatist terrorism, social-revolutionary terrorism, right-wing terrorism, religious extremism (with a particular focus on non-traditional religious groups such as Aum Shinrikyo) and single-issue terrorism.[16] It also looks at whether al-Qaeda poses a nuclear threat.

Nationalists/separatists

There is a widely held belief that nationalist-separatist groups are constrained from mass-casualty terrorism, especially nuclear terrorism, by the 'values of their base constituency', the risks of an 'an overwhelming international backlash', and a desire for international support for their cause.[17] Militant separatists have traditionally attacked clearly identified elements of the 'oppressor regime', such as military or police bases, national infrastructure or government offices, rather than civilian targets, and they have usually been careful to avoid, or at least minimise, civilian casualties. According to Post: 'Nationalist-separatist groups operating within their nation are particularly sensitive to the responses of their internal constituency, as well as their international audience. This provides a constraint against acts so violent or extra-normal as to offend their constituents.'[18] Paul Arthur has argued that the IRA 'was always very, very conscious that it had to be careful how it used its violence. It is worth pointing out that Belfast, for example, never became Beirut. There was a control to most of the violence. Before the violence occurred, there were usually plenty of warnings. Very rarely could you put [sic] your finger and say that innocent people were targeted deliberately. They were very conscious in their propaganda of how they sold their violence. They were always conscious they had to bring their people with them.'[19] To illustrate the risks of alienating core supporters, the Real IRA, an offshoot upset by the IRA's moves towards peace with the British, so outraged its constituency with its bombing of a shopping centre in Omagh in Northern Ireland in 1998 that it ceased operations soon afterwards.

There is nothing in this argument to suggest that nationalist-separatist militants would or should be constrained from mass-casualty or nuclear attacks against state military or paramilitary targets, as opposed to civilian ones, although such actions would probably be better described as unconventional or guerrilla warfare, rather than terrorism. In any case, there are enough examples of attacks against civilians to give the lie to a picture of these groups as idealistic separatist fighters, closely tied to a domestic constituency on whose behalf they claim to act, and following at least some of the rules of war. Of the IRA's 1,800 victims between 1969 and 1994, a third (600) were civilians. The most egregious example is probably the attack on Beslan in southern Russia in early September 2004, in which at least 334 people, many of them children, died. Two years earlier, Chechen militants seized a Moscow theatre, taking 700 people hostage. At least 170 people, including 129 hostages, were killed when Russian security forces stormed the building. In Dagestan in 1995, militants under Chechen guerrilla leader Shamil Basayev took a hospital and its 1,500 inhabitants hostage. In that incident, more than 100 died in two failed Russian assaults. Either the constraints mentioned by Post and others had no bearing on the Chechens' behaviour, or their claimed constituency's tolerance for violence was so broad as to impose few real limits.

More pragmatic calculations could influence whether a separatist group engages in mass-casualty or nuclear terrorism. Secessionist territories are, by definition, within the target state's legal boundaries, and in many cases target and constituency populations are intermingled. Israeli and Palestinian or Israeli Arab populations, for example, are either intermingled or, where separated, so close to one another that a WMD attack on one would be very likely to affect the other. In the case of nuclear weapons, the fallout plume from an explosion in any of Israel's major cities could easily reach the West Bank or Gaza. Other WMD are similarly indiscriminate. Any release of a biological agent in an Israeli city would be certain to affect Palestinians or Israeli Arabs.

The situation in Chechnya is such that extremists among secessionist forces might consider using WMD against Russia. Hundreds of thousands of Chechens have been killed or made homeless by the conflict there, and Russian forces have been accused of atrocities against Chechen fighters and civilians.[20] The Chechen capital Grozny has been reduced virtually to rubble by Russian carpet bombing. At the same time, there is no realistic prospect of a negotiated settlement. If extremist Chechen rebels felt that, under these circumstances, only a dramatic blow would force Russia to disengage, they might choose to use WMD, if they had access to such a capability. Russian and Chechen territories and populations are substantially distinct, especially in Moscow, which is in turn a long way from Grozny. A WMD attack on the heart of the Russian state would entail no direct risk of injuring Chechens in significant numbers or of affecting Chechnya itself. If Chechen leaders' calculations extended no further than the attack itself, their inclination to use WMD would have to be rated as very much higher than that of the Palestinians.

In both the Palestinian and Chechen cases, would-be WMD terrorists would have to consider the threat of massive retaliation. Not only is Israel an unambiguous – albeit undeclared – nuclear-weapon state, it typically exacts disproportionate vengeance on Palestinians in response to even moderate attacks, which might deter any sane Palestinian.[21] In the Chechen case, Moscow has repeatedly demonstrated that it is willing to use disproportionate force in dealing with domestic security threats. A nuclear attack by Chechen nationalists would provide a pretext for responding in kind and solving the Chechen problem once and for all. Even for Chechen nationalists, while there are some factors that increase the likelihood of nuclear terrorism, a sober calculation of the risks and benefits involved should show what an exceptionally dangerous move this would be.

It is possible that desperation or ideology might drive some organisations, especially those influenced by religious beliefs, beyond these rational calculations. Gary Ackerman and Laura Snyder claim that 'the more fanatic beliefs of [Islamist Palestinian] groups help make them psychologically capable of inflicting mass casualties. If the current conflict worsens and a sense of desperation sets in, individuals may become less rational. Existing shackles on their desire to use WMD – such as concerns about Palestinian casualties and popular support – may begin to fall away.'[22] The special properties of nuclear weapons may lead nationalists or separatists to seek them in an effort to accrue 'state-like' attributes, if only in the eyes of their constituents. Yet there is reason to believe that nationalists or separatists would not be first to use weapons of mass destruction, especially nuclear or radiological ones, despite the growing lethality of the tactics of some groups, and the precedents they have set in places like Beslan.

Social revolutionaries
Social-revolutionary groups, whether on the left or right of the political spectrum, are founded on the belief that the entire political and economic structure of a given state, and more usually the entire world, must be destroyed in order that a better one can be erected. To the extent that they are genuinely revolutionary, it might seem that the constraints against mass-casualty terrorism that operate on them would be low. However, Post argues that in fact they operate under some of the same constraints that influence separatists: 'they would be significantly constrained from indiscriminate acts that cause significant casualties among their own countrymen, or cause negative reactions in their domestic and international audiences. But discriminate acts against government or symbolic capitalist targets could be rationalized by these groups.'[23]

There are problems with this argument. The nature of revolutionary ideologies and their typical practitioners could easily permit or encourage terrorism on a massive scale, even if the protagonists were claiming to act on behalf of a larger constituency, such as 'the working class'. Revolutionary ideologies allow the core group to see itself as a tiny, embattled but chosen élite, custodians and implementers of a truth denied to others; they are ultimately global and all inclusive, rather than limited to a particular state or territory, and they allow almost any individuals or groups to be designated as enemy collaborators or fellow-travellers, or simply as expendable in the struggle for the greater good. Finally, the leaders of revolutionary groups are often markedly paranoid and/or have narcissistic traits or disorders, with grandiose beliefs about themselves, their mission and the ultimate rightness of their cause. It would be a mistake, therefore, to assume that they would necessarily make the same strategic and political calculations that rational nationalist separatists might. If international capitalism were the enemy, for example, a revolutionary group might have few qualms about trying to blow up Manhattan, Zurich or London.

The absence of significant international support for revolutionary movements might in itself encourage nuclear terrorism: if there are no state supporters to alienate, that potential constraint is void. Similarly, revolutionary groups might be tiny, with few or no attachments to particular people, communities or places, and therefore no particular constituencies to which to respond. Under these circumstances, the decision to go nuclear would seem, on the whole, to be more technical – can we build one, will it work, can it be concealed and delivered? – than ideological or humanitarian, while the massive social, economic and symbolic effects of a nuclear explosion would be extremely attractive, especially when they could be seen as hastening the collapse of an immoral system.

Right-wing terrorism

Right-wing terrorism has had a low profile since the events of 9/11. Yet there are risks that nuclear terrorism might emerge from the right-wing underground, perhaps especially from some of the cult-like forms found in North America. As Richard Falkenrath *et al.* point out: 'the problem of right-wing violence, while by no means new, appears to have grown worse since the mid-1980s. Internationally, an escalation in right-wing violence and fringe political agitation has been seen in England, Germany, France, Israel, Russia, and several other states of the former Soviet Union, manifested most often in racially motivated attacks on foreign residents.'[24] Timothy McVeigh's attack on the Alfred P. Murrah Federal Building in Oklahoma City in 1995 means that 'the precedent for massively destructive domestic terrorism has been set'.[25] It is also significant that this extremely destructive act was carried out by just two people with no significant organisational affiliations or external support. With that notable exception, however, most right-wing violence has been little more than thuggery on a larger scale. Targets have frequently been individual members of racial minorities or symbolic structures, such as religious buildings or ethnic cemeteries. Most incidents have been classified as hate crimes, rather than terrorism, because there is little evidence of coordination or an explicit political programme.

There is, however, another side to right-wing violence, at least in North America – a side which is explicitly anti-government, implicitly or explicitly revolutionary, and which holds some radically libertarian or anarchic views, such as the belief that the US federal government is intrinsically illegitimate. Some groups favour conspiracy theories: a popular example is the notion that the US government has been taken over by a clandestine Jewish cabal and should therefore be known as the 'Zionist Occupation Government', or ZOG. As this reference suggests, a broad strain of racism and anti-Semitism runs through many of the movements on the far right. Others fear the alleged 'internationalist' tendencies of the US government, and suspect it of collaborating with others to establish a toxic 'New World Order'. In some cases, these beliefs add up to a position that is sufficiently well elaborated to be called a revolutionary ideology. For such people, the symbolic qualities of nuclear or radiological weapons could be immensely attractive, gratifyingly confirming their own importance while placing them instantly on a par, at least in their own eyes, with their government enemies. Radiological terrorism might be especially appealing, as it requires relatively low levels of technical skill and equipment.

Religious terrorism

It is widely thought that religious extremists have the greatest potential for mass-casualty terrorism because they lack many of the political and psychological constraints that might bear upon other groups. Hoffman, for example, suggests that 'terrorism motivated either in whole or in part by a religious imperative, where violence is regarded by its practitioners as a divine duty or sacramental act, embraces markedly different means of legitimization and justification than that committed by secular terrorists; and these distinguishing features lead, in turn, to yet greater bloodshed and destruction'.[26] The specific question of Islamic mass-casualty terrorism, and more particularly whether al-Qaeda poses a credible nuclear threat, is dealt with below. This section focuses on the terrorist threat posed by cult groups and 'new religions'.

Violence by religious cults or 'new religions' has usually lacked political motives, and in recent years has been turned inwards, towards members, rather than against the outside world. It has nonetheless resulted in some cases in very large numbers of deaths. The mass suicide by more than 900 members of Jim Jones's People's Temple in Guyana in 1978 is possibly the best-known example of intra-cult violence, but there have been several other notable instances in recent history. One involved the deaths of as many as 1,000 members of Joseph Kibwetere and Credonia Wmerinde's millenarian Movement for the Restoration of the Ten Commandments in Uganda in 2000. In this case, members were burnt alive in a church, clubbed, stabbed, strangled or poisoned. In 1997, 39 members of the Heaven's Gate cult committed suicide in Rancho Santa Fe, California.

Some cults have directed violence outwards in terrorism. Followers of 'Bhagwan Shree Rajneesh' (an assumed name and title) carried out the worst bioterrorist attack in American history when they introduced cultured salmonella bacteria into the salad bars of ten restaurants in The Dalles, Oregon, in 1984. At least 751 people were made ill by the attack, but the total number may be much higher because salmonellosis is typically under-reported.[27] It is impossible to know whether the cult intended to kill – salmonella seldom does – but, given the scale of the attack, this must at least have been a recognised possibility.[28] One report suggests that Rajneesh vetoed the idea of using *Salmonella typhi*, the bacterium that causes typhoid fever, a life-threatening illness, on the grounds that, although a few fatalities would apparently have been acceptable, the purpose of the attack was to incapacitate people, and therefore lower the voter turnout in a local election in which the Rajneeshis had an interest.[29]

Aum Shinrikyo is by far the most important example of an aggressive cult. In addition to the Tokyo sarin attack in March 1995, in which 12 people died, Aum was responsible for at least three further gassings that killed a total of 19 people and injured thousands, some of them permanently, as well as an unknown number of individual murders and attempted murders. When Japanese police raided a cult building known as Satyan 7, they found 'a moderately large-scale chemical weapons production facility, designed by cult engineers, with first-rate equipment purchased over-the-counter'.[30] Although the plant was 'crude by industry standards', it was 'designed to produce sarin, not on a small terrorist scale, but in nearly battlefield quantities: thousands of kilograms a year'.[31] Aum also produced VX gas, used in at least one murder, and attempted to attack Shinjuku Station in Tokyo using a simple binary device capable of producing enough hydrogen cyanide gas 'to kill between 10,000 and 20,000 people'.[32] Aum also dabbled in bioterrorism, building three laboratories for toxin production, and tried to poison members of Japan's

Imperial Family, among others, with biological agents, including botulinum toxin, clostridium and anthrax. Unlike many other terrorist groups or movements, Aum is known to have been interested in radiological or nuclear weapons.

Aum leader Shoko Asahara (an assumed name) originally propounded a doctrine based largely on Buddhism, although it combined elements from Hinduism and Christianity, in particular a belief in Armageddon, the violent end of the world in which only an elect few would survive and be elevated to a higher state of being. Asahara began writing apocalyptic tracts in the late 1980s. Most of his predicted dates for the beginning of the war to end the world were between 1996 and 1998, but he later moved the date back to 1995. The cult's planned acts of mass-casualty terrorism were intended to precipitate the final war, a nuclear cataclysm.

Aum Shinrikyo illustrates many of the characteristics and behaviours of cults that might turn to terror. Not all of the following list, developed by Jean-Francois Mayer, applies to Aum, nor to all potentially violent religious groups, but combined it forms an interesting profile:

- 'Staging a spectacular action allows a small group to attract the attention of the world and may to some extent be intended to reach that goal.
- While opposition from the outside can reinforce tendencies in a group toward violent reactions, internal dissent and protest (or other developments inside the group) seem in many cases to have triggered the turn toward violence.
- A conflict between a religious group and the surrounding society may also contribute to violence … in the case of a fragile group, even a limited level of opposition can be perceived as unbearable.
- Apocalyptic thinking creates an atmosphere conducive to the legitimation of violence and – in some cases – terrorist actions. However, apocalyptic views in themselves do not seem to constitute a sufficient reason for violence, other factors will be at least as important.
- When religious beliefs are used for justifying violence, violent actions tend to become endowed with cosmic dimensions, and there is nothing left to restrain them.
- There is not a single factor that seems sufficient for identifying a tendency of a group toward violence. However, past cases show that violence at a low level often preceded more serious acts of violence or terrorism.'[33]

There is no certain method for assessing if a group presents a potential danger, but it seems possible to identify potential warning signs.[34] Obviously, the presence of one or two isolated factors does not indicate any special tendency towards violence. For instance, a group in an isolated commune with a charismatic leader is obviously not in itself sufficient to cause concern. But if the same leader had paranoid ideas and the group were suffering internal dissent or defection and were stockpiling arms, these would be very clear signals that something potentially dangerous was afoot.

Single-issue terrorism

A variety of single-issue groups have taken to terrorism to make their points, including eco-terrorists and other environmentalists, anti-nuclear activists, animal liberationists and 'right to life' activists. With regard to eco-terrorism, there would seem to be no reason why environmentalists might perpetrate the worst possible kind of ecological disaster by detonating a nuclear weapon or a RDD, or causing a radiation release. Speaking of potential eco-terrorist threats to the Yucca Mountain waste storage site or the Nevada Test Site, for example, Robert Futrell and Barbara G. Brents put forward a conventional argument: 'The movement is rooted in the pacifist peace movement and has expressed a clear philosophy of nonviolence that they have embodied in their actions. This long standing commitment to nonviolent ethics makes terrorist violence highly unlikely.'[35] Others argue that nuclear terrorism is not entirely inconceivable, even for anti-nuclear terrorists, although they would not necessarily be intent on causing massive casualties. Rather, they would be interested in exposing the risks of atomic energy and injuring the nuclear power industry in the process. The political goals of such groups dictate that, for the most part, they discriminate in their activities and develop operations with limited objectives, targets and scale. The possibility exists, however, that fringe groups might view an attack on a nuclear facility that resulted in a radiation leak as a prime option for illustrating to the public the dangers of nuclear power. These groups may also attack nuclear fuel or waste in storage or transit in an attempt to dramatise the environmental dangers the material poses.[36]

At the most extreme fringes of the environmentalist movement are those calling themselves 'green anarchists' or 'deep' or 'restoration' ecologists,[37] who advocate the annihilation of human civilisation so that the earth's ecology can regenerate itself without human overpopulation and industrial and technological interference. Walter Laqueur argues that they could turn to terrorism to achieve their ends,[38] while Charles Ferguson and William Potter suggest that they could try, for example, to breach a reactor's containment vessel to hasten environmental apocalypse and, like other putative nuclear eco-terrorists, alert the public to the dangers of nuclear energy.[39]

Is al-Qaeda a nuclear threat?

Al-Qaeda is unquestionably the best-known and, so far, the most destructive terrorist organisation in the world. Its psychological capacity for mass killing has been repeatedly demonstrated. It has also been interested in acquiring nuclear and radiological weapons for some time. In December 1998, bin Laden stated that: 'Acquiring weapons for the defense of Muslims is a religious duty. To seek to possess the weapons that could counter those of the infidels is a religious duty. If I have indeed acquired [nuclear] weapons, then this is an obligation I carried out and I thank God for enabling us to do that. And if I seek to acquire these weapons I am carrying out a duty. It would be a sin for Muslims not to try to possess the weapons that would prevent the infidels from inflicting harm on Muslims.'[40] Documents found in Afghanistan show that, while al-Qaeda's efforts to make nuclear weapons were far less sophisticated than known state programmes, it is determined to get them, and willing to use them.[41]

From time to time, it has been rumoured that al-Qaeda had acquired nuclear or radiological weapons. However, an 'extensive analysis of open source information and interviews with knowledgeable officials' concluded that there is 'no credible evidence that either bin Laden or al Qa'ida possesses nuclear weapons or sufficient fissile material to make them', or that the organisation had any fissile materials at all.[42] Claims that the organisation had bought a 'suitcase nuke' from the Kazakh state arsenal or from Chechen militants may simply indicate that it has been defrauded of large amounts of money.[43] There also seems to be no basis to rumours that the organisation had hired a number of ex-Soviet nuclear scientists.[44] The idea of attacking nuclear power stations was raised in the early stages of the development of the 9/11 attacks, but was vetoed, apparently by bin Laden himself.[45] As Tom Fingar, US Assistant Secretary of State for intelligence and research, has said: 'We have seen no persuasive evidence that al-Qaida has obtained fissile material or ever has had a serious and sustained program to do so. At worst, the group possesses small amounts of radiological material that could be used to fabricate a radiological dispersion device.'[46]

On the other hand, revelations about A.Q. Khan's extensive clandestine nuclear technology trading network, the close relationship between elements of the Pakistani armed forces and their Inter-Services Intelligence

Directorate (ISI) and the former Taliban/al-Qaeda regime in Afghanistan, and the strong Islamist sentiments still held by many members of the Pakistani armed forces, all suggest that, at some stage, al-Qaeda might acquire nuclear technology. The unclassified version of a CIA report to the US Congress in 2003 says that 'al-Qa'ida was engaged in rudimentary nuclear research, although the extent of its indigenous program is unclear. Outside experts, such as Pakistani nuclear engineer Bashir al-Din Mahmood may have provided some assistance to al-Qa'ida's program. Bashir, who reportedly met with Bin Ladin, discussed information concerning nuclear weapons.'[47] The most likely possibility would be the use of radiological devices. As the CIA points out: 'Al-Qa'ida's end goal is the use of CBRN to cause mass casualties; however, most attacks by the group – and especially by associated extremists – probably will be small scale, incorporating relatively crude delivery means and easily produced or obtained chemicals, toxins, or radiological substances.'[48] In an unclassified report in 2003, the CIA again expressed its concern about the risk of terrorist RDDs and attacks on the nuclear power infrastructure by al-Qaeda and other groups.[49]

Other groups, possibly inspired by or affiliated with al-Qaeda, have engaged in mass-casualty terrorism. Examples include train bombings in Madrid, Spain, in March 2004, in which 190 people died and around 1,800 were injured, and the Beslan attack. Two groups under investigation for the Madrid attacks – the Moroccan Islamist Combat Group (GICM) and Salafiya Jihadiya[50] – are both thought to be associated with al-Qaeda.[51] However, the notion of 'ideological linkage' to al-Qaeda is loose. To be Muslim and opposed, even violently opposed, to American and allied actions in the Middle East is not necessarily the same as subscribing to al-Qaeda's ideological package of strict *sharia* law, the unification of the Arab-speaking lands and the restoration of the Caliphate. It is entirely possible for a Muslim to arrive at an anti-American position without having been particularly influenced by al-Qaeda. The kind of impoverished analysis that regards all militant Muslims as 'al-Qaeda-affiliated' could lead us to ignore significant differences among groups in religious affiliation, organisation, strategies and tactics, in membership, recruitment and constituency, in technical resources and in the propensity to cause mass casualties.

Al-Qaeda and jihadist *strategy*

Most writing about terrorist strategy has discussed the 'traditional' forms, such nationalist/separatist or revolutionary terrorism. Transnational terrorism of the sort practised by al-Qaeda is relatively new and less studied. Al-Qaeda is neither separatist nor nationalist except, perhaps, in the loosest possible sense of the terms. Its goals are not the creation of a national homeland in the usual sense, and while some of its aims are clearly revolutionary, they are not limited to the overthrow of a single government, nor are they confined to a single state. Nonetheless, al-Qaeda has some of the characteristics of other terrorist organisations. It is weak, in that it is clearly incapable of mounting any form of conventional war against its enemies, such as the United States. While it is not nationalist in the traditional sense, al-Qaeda's campaign to expel foreign forces from Arabia appeals to a kind of pan-Arabic nationalism and ethnic identity that it sees as having been offended by the creation of artificial states and boundaries under Western colonial rule or high-handed dispensations. Al-Qaeda's struggle against 'the West' has also always had a strongly ethno-religious content – the West versus the Arabs, the Christian Crusaders and Jews versus the Muslims – and the organisation is explicitly anti-Semitic.

Al-Qaeda portrays itself as fighting the enemies of Islam wherever in the world they are, which increases its relative weakness. Indeed, al-Qaeda has probably aligned itself against a wider array of specific enemies than any militant group before it. They include the US and its allies, especially the UK, the governments of Saudi Arabia, Egypt and various other Arab states, Israel and the United Nations. Its political goals, as repeatedly stated by bin Laden in his *fatwas* and other writings, interviews and video and audio tapes,[52] are correspondingly grandiose:

- The withdrawal of all American and Western military forces from the Middle and Near East, especially Saudi Arabia ('the land of the two holy places'), Iraq and Afghanistan.
- An end to American support for Israel and the eventual extinction of Israel itself.
- The overthrow of Arab governments deemed corrupt or secular-ised, with a particular emphasis on the Saudi monarchy.
- The creation of a single pan-Arabian Muslim state in the Middle East under a renewed Caliphate.

While al-Qaeda has always made efforts to gain Muslim support, the organisation does not seem to have felt the need to move into an explicitly political role of mass mobilisation. In any case, a good deal of al-Qaeda's political work has unintentionally been done for it by the United States and its allies, as anti-Western sentiment throughout the Muslim world appears to be spreading and hardening since the invasion of Iraq. An international survey conducted a year after the invasion showed deep resentment against the United States and some popular support for elements of al-Qaeda's programme and its leadership.[53] Moreover, the scale of al-Qaeda's actions is such that no Muslim – or almost anyone else, for that matter – is ignorant of it, or fails to hold an opinion about it, with or without any overtly political activity in support of its cause. Al-Qaeda's theology holds that anyone who opposes it cannot be a true Muslim, and is therefore either irrelevant or an enemy, and it seems to feel no particular need to make converts. That said, al-Qaeda is not entirely insensitive to public sentiment. Ayman al-Zawahiri, the second-in-command of the al-Qaeda core, has apparently criticised Musab al-Zarqawi, the leader of an al-Qaeda-affiliated insurgent group in Iraq, for 'alienating the masses' through his use of 'highly-publicized brutal tactics like beheading hostages and bombing civilians at mosques'.[54]

Al-Qaeda's strategy can be seen as attritional: an attempt to raise the costs of Western involvement in the Middle East to unacceptable levels. It could be argued that the train bombings in Madrid in 2004 had precisely this effect. Within days of the attacks, Spain's right-wing government was ousted in elections and replaced by a socialist party that withdrew Spanish troops from Iraq and ended the country's support for the US-led coalition.[55] Arguably, al-Qaeda terrorism is having a similar effect in the United States, where two years after 9/11 many people saw a causal relationship between American behaviour in the Middle East and terrorist violence.[56] If it is the case that growing numbers of Americans believe that the US presence in the Middle East increases the threat of terrorism, and therefore believe, by inference, that an American withdrawal would diminish the threat, then al-Qaeda might conclude that more frequent and damaging attacks would intensify this tendency. It might even believe that another catastrophic attack, perhaps using a nuclear weapon, would prompt overwhelming domestic demand for the US to withdraw completely from the Middle East.

This would be a risky calculation. American policymakers have often been inclined to seek military solutions to foreign-policy problems; under the Bush administration, this tendency has become even more pronounced. Add to this the immediate drive for vengeance that would arise in both public and government circles and it becomes hard to imagine a massive terrorist attack leading to American disengagement, at least in the short term. In the longer term, however, the balance of costs and benefits may well swing towards disengagement. On this kind of calculation, a steady stream of lower-level attacks might serve al-Qaeda's interests better than less frequent but more lethal and dramatic incidents.

There is another strand to al-Qaeda thinking that must be accounted for. Al-Qaeda might be a militant organisation with a set of explicit political goals, and therefore possesses at least the potential for a rational strategy, but it is also a religious terrorist group. Religious beliefs may allow terrorists to ignore conventional moral constraints against killing, while also modifying or supplanting the more typical rationales for terrorism. In fact, it is frequently suggested that the killing of 'infidels' for its own sake is a positive religious duty, in al-Qaeda's view. As Ackerman and Snyder put it: 'extreme Islamist groups view the world through a radical lens, interpreting their religion as encouraging the use of any means possible to destroy "the Infidel"'.[57] In 1998, bin Laden issued a *fatwa*[58] calling for 'every Muslim who can do it in any country in which it is possible to do it' to kill Americans and their allies, both civilian and military, a call justified by reference to the Koran.[59] If this was or became the dominant mode of thinking among al-Qaeda's leadership, then there would be no reason, other than the potential costs to itself in terms of retaliation or loss of national hosts or sponsors, for the organisation not to use nuclear or other WMD if it were to obtain them.

Not even al-Qaeda, however, makes calls to kill Americans and its other enemies in a political void. In the 1998 *fatwa*, the injunction to kill is immediately followed by the less often quoted and explicitly political objective: 'in order to liberate the al-Aqsa Mosque [in Jerusalem] and the holy mosque [the Ka'aba in Mecca] from their grip, and in order for their armies to move out of all the lands of Islam, defeated and unable to threaten any Muslim'.[60] The document lists three reasons for attacking America: its 'occupation' of the Arabian Peninsula; the 'great devastation inflicted on the Iraqi people'; and the American wars in the region to 'serve the Jews' petty state', to 'destroy Iraq' and to 'fragment all the states of the region such as Iraq, Saudi Arabia, Egypt, and Sudan into paper statelets and through their disunion and weakness to guarantee Israel's survival and the continuation of the brutal crusade occupation of the Peninsula'.[61] These are all political.

Al-Qaeda published its religious justification for the 9/11 attacks in April 2002, in a little-known document entitled 'A Statement from Qaidat al-Jihad Regarding the Mandates of the Heroes and the Legality of the Operations in New York and Washington'. Although it 'was not published by Arabic or Western newspapers and has largely been ignored by experts', the document 'provides essential insights into the movement's religious rationale for September 11'.[62] In it, al-Qaeda's apologists argue that the organisation was fighting a defensive war against America and its allies.[63] The statement lists seven justifications for killing the 'protected people' – women, children and the elderly – who died in the attacks. They include retaliation:

'if the unbelievers have targeted Muslim women, children, and elderly, it is permissible for Muslims to respond in kind'; cases 'in which it is not possible to differentiate the protected ones from the combatants or from the strongholds'; and instances where 'the protected ones have assisted in combat, whether in deed, word, mind, or any other form of assistance'.[64] A further condition is particularly relevant to the present topic, although there is no way of knowing whether nuclear or other WMD were in the writer or writers' minds: 'Fifth: It is allowed for Muslims to kill protected ones among unbelievers when they are using heavy weapons that do not distinguish between combatants and protected ones, as the Prophet did in Taif when he attacked its people with catapults.'[65]

This statement may have been merely a cynical attempt to provide a religious exculpation for acts that the majority of Muslims would have found unacceptable. But it may also have been a genuine expression of belief. It is striking that it was probably issued to address concerns among al-Qaeda's constituency and membership – those it considers 'true' Muslims – because by its own logic al-Qaeda should have felt no need to justify itself either to its Christian and Jewish enemies or to those it considers false or apostate Muslims. If an attack that killed a small fraction of the numbers that would die in a nuclear blast required an apologia from an organisation that has always seemed arrogantly assured of the moral rectitude of its actions, there is clearly the possibility of a backlash from its supporters were it to carry out an even deadlier attack, whether by WMD or some other means.

A later document, this one a *fatwa* issued on 21 May 2003 by a Saudi cleric, Sheik Nasir bin Hamid al Fahd, is more disquieting. Entitled 'A Treatise on the Legal Status of Using Weapons of Mass Destruction against Infidels', it explicitly claims a justification in Muslim religious tradition for using 'nuclear, chemical, or biological weapons'.[66] The document uses the *hadith* (stories of what the Prophet did and said, especially what he permitted or forbade his companions and followers), as well as writings from scholars in five different traditions – the Hanafis, the Malikis, the Shafi'is, the Hanbalis and the Zahiris – along with 'other jurists'. One quotation illustrates its general tenor. 'Anyone who considers America's aggressions against Muslims and their lands during the past decades will conclude that striking her is permissible merely on the basis of the rule of treating as one has been treated. No other arguments need be mentioned. Some brothers have totaled the number of Muslims killed directly or indirectly by their weapons and come up with a figure of nearly ten million ... If a bomb that killed ten million of them and burned as much of their land as they have burned Muslims' land were dropped on them, it would be permissible, with no need to mention any other argument. We might need other arguments if we wanted to annihilate more than this number of them!'[67] Al Fahd and two colleagues, Ali al-Khudayr and Ahmad al-Khaladi, known collectively to the Arab media as the 'Takfir Sheikhs',[68] have published a number of *fatwas* and other writings supporting the Taliban and attacking the Saudi government. Al-Fahd himself has been described as 'close to al-Qaeda',[69] although it is not clear whether bin Laden actually requested the *fatwa* discussed here.

This and similar documents may have a number of functions for al-Qaeda that have little to do with the actual use of WMD. First, they are remarkably effective pieces of propaganda. While bin Laden appears to be sincere in his need for religious justification for his activities, it is also reasonable to picture him and his cronies gloating over the panicky reactions to his latest public statement, or to the latest ominous *fatwa* from an obliging cleric. To the extent that they are taken seriously, they are terrorist weapons in and of themselves: they spread fear and alarm, while prompting yet more public spending or yet further erosion of civil liberties in the name of the 'war on terror', at no cost to bin Laden's organisation. They also enhance al-Qaeda's status, from the harried rump of a once-formidable organisation to a potential nuclear power, again at no cost to itself. And finally, of course, they can be kept in reserve against the day al-Qaeda actually decides to use WMD.

In sum, al-Qaeda has a clear political agenda: it perceives itself to be fighting a defensive war against an alien aggressor, and it is sufficiently conscious of moral objections to the killing of non-combatants, especially 'protected people', to seek religious authorisation and justification for its acts. It is not simply engaging in mass-casualty terrorism as a kind of crude religious crusade. Thus, if the US were to withdraw its troops from the Middle East and cease its support for Israel and for Arab governments deemed illegitimate by al-Qaeda, it is possible that the organisation would stop attacking Americans. However, it would continue its campaign for a unified Arabia, a restored Caliphate and a revitalised Islam.

How then should we assess the likelihood that al-Qaeda would use a nuclear weapon? If bin Laden is indeed the malignant narcissist that Post suggests he is, he might feel driven to make ever-more impressive demonstrations of his power and reach, beyond anything a strictly rational strategy might require. In that case, the next obvious step would be an attack even more lethal than 9/11, and that would probably entail the use of WMD, if not necessarily a nuclear weapon. However, it is not proven that bin Laden's personality is such that he would subordinate strategy to personal goals, or that he would be allowed to pursue such a costly, difficult and risky project if the rest of the leadership were not convinced of its value. Mass-casualty terrorism has shown few signs of expelling the US from the Middle East, although survey results and other evidence suggest that American political opinion may be turning, if only slightly and slowly, towards disengagement. Al-Qaeda is in for the long haul: it is evidently ready to continue its campaign, which after all has roots that stretch back to the Crusades almost a millennium ago, for decades or longer, if necessary. Although the organisation would rightly expect the use of a nuclear weapon to precipitate an unprecedented international effort to eradicate it, with this sort of time horizon it might also believe that it could survive the onslaught while it waited for the dramatically increased costs of involvement in the Middle East to change American policy. If, however, a nuclear attack were likely to alienate core supporters because of the massive toll of 'protected people', or because of the inevitable international backlash against suspected hosts or sponsors, the organisation might indeed be more constrained against truly massive attacks than an initial analysis of religious terrorism might suggest.

CHAPTER FOUR

Terrorism and Nuclear Deterrence

Treating the question of 'going nuclear' as simply involving the most massive of mass-casualty terrorism obscures some important strategic considerations. It may well be the case that terrorists would indeed not look beyond the slaughter and disruption they could cause, the political leverage they dream of acquiring or the prestige they imagine they could accrue. However, nuclear weapons are generally perceived to be qualitatively different from others, and their use would have national and international implications beyond similarly destructive conventional attacks (although there are few conventional modes of attack available to terrorists that could match even a 'small' nuclear explosion). This raises the question of nuclear strategy and deterrence as it relates to terrorists.

It has become a cliché to say that terrorists would not be directly deterred from using nuclear weapons by the threat of nuclear retaliation because their weapons have 'no return address'. According to Admiral Richard W. Mies, commander-in-chief of US Strategic Command: 'The post-Cold War world is a more chaotic place. Strategic deterrence, which worked well in the bipolar framework of the Cold War, may not work as well in a multipolar world of unpredictable, asymmetric threats, and in some cases, it may fail. How do you deter a threat that has no return address? How do you dissuade a threat that is faceless?'[1] This argument is narrowly correct in terms of modern transnational terrorist groups, which have no single host, sponsor or homeland. However, at least two important qualifications apply. First, while terrorist groups themselves might not be directly deterred by the threat of massive retaliation, host or sponsor states might be, and indeed should be, which could have an indirect or secondary deterrent effect on militant groups. Second, it may not in fact be impossible to trace a weapon to its source.

With regard to the first point, it is sometimes speculated that a state might actively or passively help a terrorist group to acquire a nuclear weapon. It is almost inconceivable, however, that any state, of any stripe, would knowingly allow a nuclear weapon on its soil in the possession of actors that were not themselves under the state's tightest possible control and hence effectively part of it, if for no other reason than the fear that the weapon might be used against itself. Nor could it allow the expertise and physical plant required to build one to be outside of state control. Why sponsor a nuclear programme if the state were not the primary beneficiary? In the case of second-tier nuclear-weapon states, the weapons themselves are national treasures, bought at great cost, invested with immense symbolic value and therefore presumably kept under tight control. (The A.Q. Kahn episode is evidence of a state entity sharing some nuclear technology – but possibly not fissile materials and certainly not bombs – with other friendly states, not terrorists.) If state-sponsored nuclear terror were to occur, it would most probably be a case of a state using an unconventional delivery system, a potentially attractive option if the attack were thought to be deniable or if the state lacked suitable delivery vehicles, such as intercontinental ballistic missiles. That, at any rate, is how it would be seen by the victim and the international community.

The possibility that a terrorist weapon could be traced back to the sponsor, even if relatively low, should still be too high in relation to the worst possible consequences – nuclear annihilation – for a state to sponsor or even knowingly to host nuclear terrorists. Even passive, unwitting hosts might face some level of retaliation if it could be argued that they *should* have known about the terrorists on their soil. *All* nuclear-weapon states – established, 'rogue' and clandestine proliferators alike – have the strongest possible interests in ensuring that terrorists do not get hold of nuclear weapons and, therefore, in maintaining control of their nuclear materials and technology. This is, of course, especially true since the enunciation of the so-called First Bush Doctrine, in which US President George W. Bush announced that the United States would 'make no distinction between the terrorists who committed [the 9/11 attacks] and those who harbour them'.[2]

Not all states or their leaderships are necessarily rational, of course, but it is still difficult to imagine any state actively sponsoring nuclear terrorism. Both the obvious potential candidates, Iran and North Korea, have engaged in risky nuclear brinkmanship, but it is highly unlikely that either would sponsor a terrorist nuclear attack on another state. North Korea has consistently used its nuclear programme as a way of wringing concessions from the West, and even as erratic a ruler as Kim Jong Il would not launch a nuclear attack of any sort unless he were *in extremis*, facing an imminent invasion by the combined forces of the US and South Korea, perhaps, or confronting the collapse of his regime for other reasons. Under those circumstances, however, he would be unlikely to deliver his weapons clandestinely. For Iran, the possible pursuit of a nuclear-weapon programme has increased international pressure and prompted hints of military intervention; sponsoring a nuclear attack would simply seal the country's fate. The risk is compounded by the fact that the wounded party might not be over-concerned with proof of sponsorship. The most likely target, the United States, has invaded two countries and toppled their governments, inflicting thousands of casualties in the process, largely because of these states' associations, proven in one case but merely assumed in the other, with an attack that killed 3,000 Americans. How might it respond to an attack that killed perhaps half a million citizens, devastated Manhattan or Washington and crippled the national and global economies?

The second issue concerns determining the source of the bomb itself. This would be a difficult and complex process, though known techniques would at least considerably narrow the range of possibilities. A detailed chemical and radiological analysis of the fallout would reveal a good deal about the fissile materials and bomb components. By 1995, Lawrence Livermore Laboratories had begun developing techniques for tracing terrorist nuclear weapons back to their origins. These include mass spectrometry of fissile-material and bomb fragments, which would reveal components or impurities, including tritium, U-240, neptunium, americium, gadolinium, curium and promethium, found in the plutonium or HEU core of the weapon.[3] The IAEA keeps detailed records, including the ratios and types of isotopes present in each batch, of fissile materials produced under its safeguards, and these would assist in this tracing work. However, these records exclude production by the five original nuclear powers, as well as by non-signatories to the NPT, such as Pakistan, India, Israel and North Korea; obviously, they also do not cover clandestine operations. Still, as David Rothberg points out, IAEA records, as well as any information supplied by the five established nuclear states, would be helpful in excluding certain sources, while other techniques could indicate how the material was enriched and, perhaps, where the original uranium had been mined.[4]

Any country that did not promptly provide its records, or claimed not to have any, would immediately come under threat of nuclear retaliation.

Estimating the bomb's explosive yield would be relatively straight-forward, although its value as evidence would be ambiguous. Improvised nuclear devices (INDs) are likely to be in the low kiloton to sub-kiloton range, and would probably be particularly 'dirty' and inefficient. Even the combination of low yield and inefficiency would not suffice to prove that the weapon had not come from a state, however. A state launching a clan-destine attack on another, or allowing terrorists to do so, would do well to disguise its weapon as an IND.

The situation would be particularly dangerous and delicate in South Asia, where three nuclear powers, Pakistan, India and China, all with long and complex histories of mutual antagonism, confront each other across disputed borders. India and Pakistan frequently accuse one another of fomenting or carrying out terrorism on one another's territories. If one of these states were thought to be behind a 'terrorist' nuclear attack in the region, the risks of the incident escalating into a full nuclear exchange would be high.

Whether the victim state were nuclear armed or not, and quite apart from the practical problems of identifying and locating the bombers and their hosts or sponsors, the victim would still have to consider the claim, which might well ensue, that the bombers had more than one device, and decide on its response in that light. The most worrying scenario would be one in which terrorists claimed responsibility for the first bomb, said that they had more weapons, and claimed that they had been pre-positioned, ready to detonate, in various cities.[5] A government might be able to make informed estimates of the plausibility of the claim. For example, if the bomb were detonated after a detected theft of a weapons-useable quantity of fissile material, analysis of the first blast could suggest whether enough remained to make another bomb. However, fissile materials around the world are still insecure enough that this might not be sufficient in itself to adequately assess the claim.

It is worth speculating briefly on the likely consequences should terror-ists claim that they had pre-positioned a second nuclear bomb, to illustrate the issues that a government would have to consider. It may not be neces-sary for a public announcement of a threat to other cities even to be made – simple panic and the reasonable belief that 'if it happened to New York (or London or Moscow), it could happen here too' could be enough. First, there would be an immediate and disorderly evacuation of other major cities. Air, rail and road traffic would be brought to a standstill, services and public utilities would collapse and martial law would be declared. Civil liberties, including press freedom, would be suspended. Empty city centres would be patrolled against looters, while over-extended nuclear-emergency teams attempted to scan all of them for signs of other bombs. Supplies of food, water and energy would begin to break down, and health conditions in the enormous tent cities that would appear outside urban centres would rapidly decline from merely squalid to positively danger-ous. The repercussions on global markets, already battered by the initial blast, would be devastating.

Under these circumstances, the culprits might be tempted to make immoderate demands. Brian Jenkins, however, claims that 'translating the enormous coercive power that a nuclear weapon would give a terror-ist group into concrete political gains … poses some difficulties'.[6] Jenkins argues that governments simply could not comply with some essentially impossible demands, such as their own dissolution: 'Nor could terrorists enforce permanent policy changes unless they maintained the threat indef-initely. And if a government could not be assured that the threat would be dismantled once the demands were met, it would have little incentive to negotiate … I am suggesting that it is not easy for terrorists, even if they are armed with nuclear weapons, to achieve lasting political results. They might find nuclear weapons to be as useless as they are powerful.'[7]

This argument is not entirely convincing. It might apply to the developed states that are the likely targets of nuclear terrorism, if the terrorists were indeed making impossible demands. However, if the terrorist group was al-Qaeda, for example, and the demand was that the US remove its troops from the Middle East and cease its military and financial support for Israel, the US could comply, high though the political costs of doing so would be. Deciding to set a precedent that states could be blackmailed by terrorists would be a difficult decision to take, however, even if thousands or millions of lives were at stake. Furthermore, some weak states – in Africa, perhaps – could succumb to the threat of nuclear destruction and essentially hand government over to the terrorists. While such states would not be the first targets of nuclear terrorists, they might be tempting as potential havens after a nuclear attack. If the terrorists restricted themselves to demands that a state keep their presence secret and provided a modest level of support, they might be safe for some time, especially if the state in question had been of little interest to the international media or intelligence agencies.

In any case, nuclear terrorists might not be interested in political lever-age of the kind Jenkins mentions. Their only goal might be to inflict the most massive possible damage on a target society or, in the case of an apocalyptic movement, to precipitate a full-scale global nuclear war. Religiously motivated groups are the most likely to be interested in destruction more-or-less for its own sake, although any political leverage they would accrue would certainly be exploited to the full.

While they might consider themselves relatively immune from direct nuclear retaliation, terrorists would still have to consider the consequences to them of any attack. On the one hand, no state could possibly risk being identified as a host or sponsor of the attackers, especially if a nuclear power or a state under the protection of one had been targeted, and so would be obliged to make the most strenuous and visible efforts to root out the attackers. Even nascent nuclear states with no love for the West, such as Iran and North Korea, would surely not be willing to risk annihilation as the cost of protecting terrorists. On the other hand, many states would simply lack the capacity to find and disable terrorist groups, and could unwillingly or unwittingly provide a safe haven more-or-less indefinitely. Even the United States, some years into a full-scale, extremely costly 'war on terror', has been unable to kill or capture all of al-Qaeda's leadership, despite its invasions of Afghanistan and Iraq and the cooperation of Pakistan.

Conclusion

Addressing the question of whether terrorists would go nuclear is an all-but impossible task. If one discounts the argument that the two instances of atomic bombing in the Second World War were state nuclear terrorism, there are no cases to study and there is no historical evidence to unearth. Neither terrorists nor those who fight them, especially government counter-terrorism agencies, are particularly prone to disseminating credible, concrete information in the public realm. While it may be possible to understand, even empathise with, terrorists in order to come to a roughly plausible approximation of their moral, strategic and political beliefs, we are in the end left with 'what-if' and 'best-guess' thinking: speculation, in a word.

Nonetheless, there is considerable evidence that must inform this speculation and narrow its range. First, there are technical considerations. Assembling enough fissile material for even the crudest nuclear device – and the amounts needed vary inversely with sophistication – would be very difficult and probably extremely expensive for a terrorist organisation. The theoretical knowledge and practical skills required to design and build a nuclear weapon are of a high order, while setting up, equipping and successfully operating an undetectable clandestine weapons laboratory would be difficult and expensive, even for the best-funded terrorist organisation. Aum Shinrikyo, which operated relatively openly under Japanese laws regarding religious organisations that made it all-but-untouchable, and which had a billion-dollar war chest, gave up the attempt to develop a nuclear weapon very early on in the process, preferring to work with chemical and biological agents instead. The evidence, much of it admittedly negative, suggests that buying or stealing a functional nuclear weapon would be an even more difficult, perhaps impossible, task. Nuclear weapons are guarded like national treasures; indeed, nuclear weapons *are* in some sense national treasures, symbols of national strength and modernity bought at immense cost. No state that possessed them, whether established or 'rogue', would be likely to hand over such weapons to terrorists unless they were acting as mercenary agents of the state itself. The threat of nuclear retaliation, even if the possibility of tracing the weapon back to its source were thought to be low, should be enough to deter any rational state from using a nuclear weapon against another nuclear-weapon state, or a country under the protection of one.

Leaving aside the technical issue, there remains the question of whether terrorists would use nuclear weapons if they somehow managed to obtain them. Terrorist organisations vary among themselves at least as much as any other set of broadly comparable human institutions – religions, for example, or tribes. In other words, they have different goals, different histories, different leaderships and leadership styles, different cultural roots, different political contexts, different sets of moral beliefs and constraints and different strategies. Nonetheless, it is possible to distinguish between several broad categories of terrorist organisation, such as social revolutionary, nationalist-separatist and religious.

Of these types, apocalyptic religious or cultist terrorists are the most dangerous, from a purely motivational and strategic viewpoint. These organisations believe that they have a direct divine mandate. As such, they recognise no secular legal or moral constraints on their actions and do not answer to an earthly constituency, while the promise of immediate heavenly reward means that self-preservation itself has no value, making void any possibility of deterrence. Their political agendas, to the extent that they have any, are typically both vague and grandiose; in the most threatening form, they believe that human civilisation itself must be destroyed so that a new order, usually populated or led by members of the cult, can emerge. With Aum Shinrikyo, the world probably came as close as it ever has to true nuclear terrorism. No other cult is known to have approached its wealth and technical resources, but any apocalyptic cult poses a threat to the security of its host state and, eventually, the world. This threat increases as it amasses wealth and power. With the exception of authoritarian countries, where they have been persecuted as 'threats to state security', religious groups have not traditionally attracted as much attention from security agencies as more typical terrorist organisations. While the fight against terrorism must be carefully balanced against the need to respect civil rights, including religious freedom, the lesson of Aum Shinrikyo must also be taken to heart.

The next most dangerous form of terrorism is the religiously inspired transnational variety uniquely exemplified by al-Qaeda. While al-Qaeda is not apocalyptic and has more narrow and better-defined political goals than a cult such as Aum Shinrikyo, it has some characteristics of a purely religious terrorist group. Specifically, it claims a religious justification for its actions, and says that killing its enemies, which it generically calls 'infidels', is a positive religious duty that will be rewarded in the hereafter. It has also demonstrated its practical and psychological ability to engage in mass-casualty terrorism. Unlike cults, however, al-Qaeda has a broader constituency beyond its membership, on which it relies for support and towards which it appears to feel at least some moral obligation. It locates its struggle in the concrete world of real political actors, not in a more abstract spiritual realm; the outcomes it desires are equally concrete, and to the extent that it engages in strategic thinking, it does so in response to the configurations and dynamics of power in the real world. Al-Qaeda, therefore, is not as utterly unconstrained from mass-casualty terrorism as a cult like Aum Shinrikyo might have been. At the same time, however, al-Qaeda can easily differentiate, on ethnic grounds, its target populations from those on whose behalf the organisation claims to be acting. Its potential targets for nuclear terrorism are far from its heartlands in the Near and Middle East, and the chances of killing significant members of its core constituency in such an attack are very low. It might also believe that its transnational nature would provide a level of immunity to retaliation, hence its alleged undeterrability.

Nationalist-separatist terrorists are, on the whole, less likely than a group such as al-Qaeda to engage in nuclear terrorism. In these cases, the terrorists are claiming to act on behalf of a clearly defined, relatively small constituency on whom they depend not only for material support but also for whatever legitimacy they might have. They would therefore be significantly constrained against mass-casualty terrorism to the extent that their constituency harboured moral or other objections (such as the fear of retaliation). Groups such as these frequently rely on overt or covert sponsorship by states, although state support for terrorism has declined significantly in recent years with the end of the Cold War and attempts by states such as Libya to rehabilitate themselves in the international community. Nonetheless, if this sponsorship existed it could be another powerful source of constraint. Finally, in these cases the claimed national homeland is by definition a part of the target state, and the target and constituency populations either live close together or are commingled. This would be another check on the use of weapons of mass destruction, which are by their nature indiscriminate.

There are, however, cases where these moral and tactical constraints would not apply as strongly, and possibly not at all. Chechen separatists consider themselves oppressed by Russian imperialists and colonisers whose 'headquarters', Moscow, is far from Chechnya, and the two populations are quite distinct. Chechnya has been victimised in two wars to repress separatism, while the Chechens have never truly acceded to Russian rule and anti-Russian sentiment runs deep, suggesting that the Chechen population might be inured to violence, and might have few inhibitions against killing Russians in large numbers. There is an alliance of sorts between Chechen separatists led by Shamil Basayev and al-Qaeda, although it is hard to say whether this is a marriage of convenience, or whether it reflects true *jihadi* sentiments among the separatists. Whatever the case, Basayev's organisation has a consistent record of taking very large numbers of hostages in incidents that have ended with correspondingly large numbers of casualties, albeit chiefly at the hands of Russian forces. All these factors would seem to point to a higher risk of nuclear terrorism. They must, however, be balanced against the fact that, unlike transnational *jihadists*, nationalist-separatist terrorists have distinct homelands and population bases that would be vulnerable to retaliation. In the case of a Chechen nuclear attack on a Russian target, for example, nuclear retaliation against Chechnya would be a strong possibility.

Finally, there are the potential wild cards: actors such as single-issue groups, right-wing extremists or ideological revolutionary terrorists. Groups such as these are often small, mobile and little known, and might be peculiarly prone to developing apocalyptic ideologies and cult-like behaviour. With the present international focus on al-Qaeda and its affiliates, there is a risk that they may develop some form of WMD capability, while being almost completely ignored by security agencies. It is extremely unlikely that such small groups could obtain true nuclear weapons, but the risks of their using radiological devices could be high.

It is important to remember that terrorists, with the possible exception of al-Qaeda, are not known for their great tactical innovation. The traditional tools of terrorism – hostage-taking, bombings, shoot-and-run sniper attacks – have only relatively recently been expanded to include the use of suicide bombers, and even suicide bombs are only a particularly unpleasant and vicious variation on an older theme. Terrorists in general probably share the same ignorance and fear of WMD prevalent in the broader population, and probably see little reason to turn to unknown, possibly unpredictable and certainly dangerous substances and techniques when the older tactics have proved themselves to be simple, reliable and cheap – or so, at least, we hope.

Dirty Bombs: Radiological Dispersal and Emission Devices

- Practically any state or non-state actor can build and detonate radiation dispersal devices (RDDs) as technological barriers have been removed and radiological materials have become more plentiful. However, weapon-design experts contend that the physical threat from these RDDs may be overstated.
- The psychological and political effects of RDDs are not well understood, and are potentially more significant than their lethality.
- While RDDs may not be 'military weapons' in the classic sense, they could be powerfully coercive and could trigger enormous political reactions within host countries or among allies in a coalition. These reactions could produce major strategic consequences for the military campaign.[1]

Terrorists are much more likely to deploy RDDs or radiation emission devices (REDs) than true nuclear weapons. It is generally acknowledged that, in most plausible scenarios, such weapons would pose little material threat to the public, and that any associated fatalities would arise either from the direct effects of the blast, or would appear as a small, and possibly statistically insignificant, increase in cancer deaths among the affected population.

Radiation dispersal devices are much easier to build and deliver than true nuclear weapons. All one needs is a radiation source and a means of distributing the radiation. The first may not be much of an obstacle to determined terrorists, and the second certainly is not. The typical RDD is a home-made device, perhaps a pipe or fertilizer bomb, incorporating radioactive material that would be powdered or vaporised by the blast. This could be effective, but it is not the only way, nor even necessarily the best way, of spreading radiation. One could simply drop an unshielded radiation source near a pedestrian bottleneck, such as an entrance to a subway station or stadium, and allow people to irradiate and re-irradiate themselves. To the naked eye, there would be nothing to distinguish the radiation source from a chunk of scrap metal, and it could remain in place for a long time before epidemiological techniques traced its location.

Non-fissile radiation sources used in commercial, industrial and medical facilities are kept under significantly lower security than reactor fuels or military materials, and are particularly dangerous because they were created for the express purpose of generating intense ionising radiation.[2] The Center for Nonproliferation Studies (CNS) states that 'tens of thousands' of the millions of commercial radiation sources worldwide 'pose inherently high security risks because of their portability, dispersability, and higher levels of radioactivity'.[3] In the United States, as many as 375 radiation sources became orphaned, or 'lost to institutional control', in a single year, and only a little more half, on average, are ever recovered.[4]

Only seven to nine radioisotopes are generally considered potentially usable in RDD/REDs. According to the Argonne National Laboratory at the University of Chicago, they are:

- americium-241 (Am^{241})
- californium-252 (Cf^{252})
- cesium-137 (Cs^{137})
- cobalt-60 (Co^{60})
- iridium-192 (Ir^{192})
- plutonium-238 (Pu^{238})
- polonium-210 (Po^{210})
- radium-226 (Ra^{226})
- strontium-90 (Sr^{90})[5]

Ferguson et al. do not include Ra^{226} and Po^{210} in their list of RDD candidate substances.[6]

Despite the risks arising from the various kinds of 'loose' radioactive materials around the world, there has been little evidence that terrorists have or would use them. So far, there has been only one significant terrorist incident involving radioactive materials: Chechen separatists placed an

RDD containing an unknown amount of cesium-137 in a Moscow park in 1995. A Chechen rebel leader alerted the media and the bomb was never detonated, so the incident amounted to a publicity stunt, albeit a rather dangerous one.

There is considerable debate about the military utility of RDDs, although the consensus appears to be that they would be better termed weapons of mass disruption, rather than mass destruction. Even if the radiation dose delivered by an RDD were negligible, the popular fear of anything associated with radiation would cause widespread panic, which could be almost as damaging to public morale and economic activity as a truly lethal device. If it became publicly known that an RDD had been detonated in a city, an immediate disorderly attempt by the panic-stricken populace to evacuate would probably follow.

Despite the low probable lethality of most foreseeable RDDs, certain radioisotopes, such as cobalt-60, a powerful emitter of gamma radiation, might be quite destructive. The isotope is widely used in food irradiation and elsewhere, and is usually supplied in the form of rods or 'pencils' a foot long and a maximum of four inches in diameter. In 2002, the Federation of American Scientists (FAS) prepared a number of RDD scenarios for the US Senate Committee on Foreign Relations. One, involving the detonation of an RDD containing a single cobalt-60 rod in Manhattan, concluded that the contamination would be comparable to that caused by the Chernobyl reactor meltdown. 'An area of approximately one-thousand square kilometers, extending over three states, would be contaminated' and 'it would be decades before the city was inhabitable again, and demolition might be necessary'.[7] These conclusions are, however, controversial. The American Nuclear Regulatory Commission (NRC) took issue with some of them, especially the claim that the worst-contaminated areas would have to be condemned. Cobalt-60 is a relatively short-lived isotope, with a half-life of only 5.27 years. Even if an area were heavily contaminated, less than 1% of the isotope would remain radioactive after less than 40 years.[8] Again, however, public prejudice might play a role. Even if an area were technically safe, there might be political pressure to place it permanently off-limits.

Another source also questions the lethality of a small cobalt-60 RDD, but introduces a truly frightening scenario: a truck bomb carrying '50 kilograms of bundled, not ground, one-year-old spent fuel rods': 'An RDD constructed using [5,000 curies of] Co-60 would produce a maximum dosage at the point of detonation of 12 rem (Roentgen Man Equivalent), resulting in no radiation related deaths. In marked contrast, the RDD made from spent reactor fuel would result in a maximum dosage at the point of detonation of 3,064 rem (six times the lethal dosage). The detonation could produce a circle of potential lethal dosage extending about a kilometer ... and a significant amount of radioactive material would remain at the detonation site'.[9]

Notes

Introduction

1 Karl-Heinz Kamp, 'An Overrated Nightmare', *Bulletin of the Atomic Scientists*, vol. 52, no. 4, July–August 1996, pp. 30–35.

2 See the detailed mathematical discussion of many aspects of nuclear-weapon design presented by Carey Sublette in 'Elements of Fission Weapon Design', Nuclear Weapons Archive, http://nuclearweaponarchive. org/Nwfaq/Nfaq4-1.html#Nfaq4.1.

3 Gavin Cameron, 'Nuclear Terrorism Reconsidered', *Current History*, vol. 99, no. 636, April 2000, p. 154.

Chapter One

1 After Robin Frost, 'Nuclear Terrorism Post 9-11: Assessing the Risks', *Global Society*, vol. 18, no. 4, October 2004.

2 Director of Central Intelligence (DCI), *Annual Report to Congress on the Safety and Security of Russian Nuclear Facilities and Military Forces 2002*, National Intelligence Council (NIC), February 2002, p. 8, http://www.cia.gov/nic/PDF_GIF_otherprod/russiannucfac.pdf.

3 International Atomic Energy Agency (IAEA), 'The IAEA Illicit Trafficking Database (ITDB) – Fact Sheet for 1993–2004', http://www.iaea.org/NewsCenter/Features/RadSources/fact_figures2004.pdf.

4 Lyudmila Zaitseva and Kevin Hand, 'Nuclear Smuggling Chains: Suppliers, Intermediaries, and End-Users', *American Behavioral Scientist*, vol. 46, no. 6, February 2003, p. 824.

5 *Ibid.*, p. 825.

6 See 'Confiscated Uranium May Be Part of a Lost Fuel Assembly', *Nuclear News*, February 1995, p. 63, abstracted by the NTI, http://www.nti.org/db/nistraff/1995/19950200.htm.

7 HEU contains 20% or more uranium-235 (U^{235}), the most important fissile isotope of uranium (U^{233} is the other); LEU contains less than 20%. Uranium is enriched using various technologies, most commonly ultra-high speed gas centrifuges, to separate the U^{235} from the rest, which is then known as depleted uranium (DU). Most nuclear reactors use LEU enriched to around 3–5%, although some can use the natural, unenriched metal. Weapons-grade uranium contains at least 90% U^{235}, although the term is sometimes reserved for 94% and higher HEU. Weapons have been made with lower levels of enriched uranium.

8 Plutonium-239 (Pu^{239}) is the chief fissile isotope of plutonium. It occurs in nature, but is extremely rare. All Pu^{239} used in weapons or elsewhere is manufactured by irradiating uranium in nuclear reactor

cores. Plutonium occurs in other isotopes, such as Pu^{240}, but the even-numbered isotopes have properties that make them undesirable as nuclear-weapon fuel.

9   IAEA, 'The IAEA Illicit Trafficking Database'.

10 Igor Andryushin, Sergey Safronov and Yuri Yudin (eds), *Nuclear Technologies and Non-Proliferation Policies Digest*, Issue 4 (Sarov: Analytical Center for Non-Proliferation Studies, 2001), http://npc.sarov.ru/english/digest/42001/appendix4.html, Annex 4.

11 J. Carson Mark *et al.*, 'Can Terrorists Build Nuclear Weapons?', in Paul Leventhal and Yonah Alexander (eds), *Preventing Nuclear Terrorism* (Lexington, MA/Toronto: Lexington Books, 1987), p. 57.

12 MOX, or mixed-oxide reactor fuel, is produced as a way of using the plutonium created when reactor fuel is irradiated in a reactor core, and to improve the overall energy extraction from uranium. It consists of 7% plutonium oxide mixed with depleted uranium, also in the form of an oxide.

13 Mark Hibbs, 'Plutonium Powder Puzzles Police', *Bulletin of the Atomic Scientists*, September 1994, pp. 6–7, http://www.nti.org/db/nuclear/1994/n9411702.htm.

14 Andryushin *et al.*, *Nuclear Technologies*, Annex 4. Lyudmila Zaitseva and Kevin Hand state that the material stolen was only 21% U^{235} (highly enriched, technically, but just barely so). Zaitseva and Hand, 'Nuclear Smuggling Chains', p. 822.

15 DCI, *Annual Report to Congress on the Safety and Security of Russian Nuclear Facilities and Military Forces*, Central Intelligence Agency (CIA), December 2004, http://www.cia.gov/nic/PDF_GIF_otherprod/russiannuke04.pdf, p. 8.

16 *Ibid.*, p. 8.

17 William C. Potter, 'Nuclear Leakage from the Post-Soviet States', Oral Presentation Before the Permanent Subcommittee on Investigations, US Senate Committee on Governmental Affairs, 13 March 1996, http://cns.miis.edu/pubs/reports/senoral.htm.

18 Rensselaer W. Lee III, *Smuggling Armageddon: The Nuclear Black Market in the Former Soviet Union* (New York: St Martin's Press, 1998), cited in Zaitseva and Hand, 'Nuclear Smuggling Chains', p. 829.

19 IAEA, 'The IAEA Illicit Trafficking Database'.

20 See George Bunn and Matthew Bunn, 'Reducing the Threat of Nuclear Theft and Sabotage', paper delivered at an IAEA symposium, 30 October 2001, http://www.iaea.org/NewsCenter/Features/Nuclear_Terrorism/bunn02.pdf. For more on the Congo reactor, see Michela Wrong, 'More Wreck than Reactor', *Financial Times*, 21 August 1999, p. 8, abstracted by the Nuclear Threat Initiative (NTI), http://www.nti.org/db/nistraff/1999/19990690.htm.

21 John Deutch, quoted in Lee, *Smuggling Armageddon*, p. 19.

22 Lee, *Smuggling Armageddon*, p. 19.

23 Rensselaer W. Lee III, quoted in Representative John Linder, chair, 'Hearing of the Subcommittee on Prevention of Nuclear and Biological Attack of the House Committee on Homeland Security – Subject: "Trends In Illicit Movement Of Nuclear Materials"', *Federal News Service*, 22 September 2005, Lexis/Nexis, http://www6.lexisnexis.com/ publisher/EndUser?Action=UserDisplayFullDocument&orgId=685&topicId=14288&docId=l:313296318&start=1.

24 Deutch, quoted in Lee, *Smuggling Armageddon*, p. 19

25 Zaitseva and Hand, 'Nuclear Smuggling Chains', p. 824.

26 *Ibid.*

27 Lee, *Smuggling Armageddon*, pp. 124–25. See also Gavin Cameron, *Nuclear Terrorism: A Threat Assessment for the 21st Century* (New York: St Martin's Press, 1999), pp. 5, 8.

28 Joseph Cirincione, Director for Non-Proliferation at the Carnegie Endowment for International Peace, quoted in Ross Liemer, 'Expert Warns of Risk from Leftover Soviet Arsenal', *Daily Princetonian*, 5 April 2005.

29 Benjamin Friedman, 'International Cooperation on Nuclear Security Still

Lacks Urgency', Center for Defense Information (CDI), 22 January 2003, http://www.cdi.org/nuclear/cooperation.cfm.

30 Paul Richter, 'Tactical Nuclear Weapons Pose Major Concern', *Detroit News*, 25 May 2005, http://www.detnews.com/2002/nation/0205/25/nation-498888.htm.

31 These sites include Chelyabinsk-65, known as 'Mayak', Krasnoyarsk-26, Krasnoyarsk-45, Tomsk-7 and Sverdlovsk-44; the nuclear-weapon laboratories Arzamas-16 and Chelyabinsk-70; and weapon assembly/disassembly sites including Penza-19, Sverdlovsk-45 and Zlatoust-36.

32 Lee, *Smuggling Armageddon*, p. 2.

33 Amy F. Woolf, 'Issue Brief 91144: Nuclear Weapons in the Former Soviet Union: Location, Command, and Control', Congressional Research Service, Foreign Affairs and National Defense Division, updated 27 November 1996, reproduced by the FAS, http://www.fas.org/spp/starwars/crs/91-144.htm.

34 Jon Brook Wolfstahl, Cristina-Astrid Chuen and Emily Ewell Daughtry (eds), *Nuclear Status Report: Nuclear Weapons, Fissile Material, and Export Controls in the Former Soviet Union*, no. 6 (Monterey, CA and Washington DC: Center for Nonproliferation Studies and Carnegie Endowment for International Peace, 2001), p. 32.

35 Russian nuclear forces profile generated by the Stockholm International Peace Research Institute (SIPRI), Facts on International Relations and Security Trends (FIRST) Database, 5 August 2005, from data in the *SIPRI Yearbooks*, 1999–2004, Nuclear Arms Control (first.sipri.org).

36 William Potter and Nikolai Sokov, 'Tactical Nuclear Weapons: The Nature of the Problem', report initially prepared for a discussion session on tactical nuclear weapons organised by the UN Institute for Disarmament Research (UNDIR), Geneva, 21–22 March 2000, http://cns.miis.edu/pubs/reports/tnw_nat.htm#_ftn1.

37 DCI, *Annual Report to Congress on the Safety and Security of Russian Nuclear Facilities and Military Forces*, 2002, p. 3.

38 *Ibid.*, p. 6.

39 DCI, *Annual Report to Congress on the Safety and Security of Russian Nuclear Facilities and Military Forces*, 2004, p. 6.

40 '12th Main Directorate (Glavnoye Upravleniye Ministerstvo Oborony)' globalsecurity.org, http://www.globalsecurity.org/wmd/world/russia/12gumo.htm. Translated from the Russian.

41 DCI, *Annual Report to Congress*, 2002, p. 7.

42 *Ibid.*, p. 6.

43 *Ibid.*

44 *Ibid.*

45 Graham Allison, *Nuclear Terrorism: The Ultimate Preventable Catastrophe* (New York: Times Books, 2004), p. 69.

46 *Ibid.*

47 DCI, *Annual Report to Congress*, 2002, p. 5.

48 DCI, *Annual Report to Congress*, 2004, p. 6. Adamov was arrested in Switzerland on 5 May 2005, at the request of US authorities who accused him of embezzling $9m from US Department of Energy funds intended to improve safety at Russian nuclear sites. 'Swiss To Extradite Russian Ex-nuclear Minister to USA', *Bellona Foundation*, 3 October 2005, http://www.bellona.no/en/international/russia/nuke_industry/co-operation/40064.html. The possibility that Adamov is a thief does not necessarily affect the accuracy of his statements about nuclear security.

49 Nikolai Sokov, '"Suitcase Nukes": A Reassessment', Center for Nonproliferation Studies, Monterey Institute of International Studies, 23 September 2002, http://cns.miis.edu/pubs/week/020923.htm.

50 *Ibid.*

51 Daly, Parachini and Rosenau, *Aum Shinrikyo*, p. 17.

52 Linda Bilmes, Kennedy School of Government, Harvard University, quoted in David R. Francis, 'More Costly than "The War To End All Wars"', *Christian Science Monitor*, 29 August 2005, http://www.csmonitor.com/2005/0829/p15s01-cogn.html.

53 Allison, *Nuclear Terrorism*, p. 177.

Chapter Two

1   Luis Alvarez, quoted in Alan J. Kuperman, 'Loose Nukes of the West', *Washington Post*, 7 May 2003, http://www.nci.org/index.htm, p. A31.

2   Allison, *Nuclear Terrorism*, p. 93.

3   Cameron, *Nuclear Terrorism*, p. 131.

4   Mark *et al.*, 'Can Terrorists Build Nuclear Weapons?', pp. 58–9.

5   See John Holdren and Matthew Bunn, 'A Tutorial on Nuclear Weapons and Nuclear-Explosive Materials – Part Two: Types of Nuclear Bombs, and the Difficulty of Making Them', footnotes 7 and 19, Nuclear Threat Initiative (NTI), http://www.nti.org/e_research/cnwm/overview/technical2.asp#_ftn4.

6   Friedrich Steinhausler, 'What It Takes To Become a Nuclear Terrorist', *American Behavioral Scientist*, vol. 46, no. 6, February 2003, p. 792.

7   Mark *et al.*, 'Can Terrorists Build Nuclear Weapons?', p. 56.

8   *Ibid.*

9   See Lawrence Livermore National Laboratory, 'Nuclear Science: A First Look at Plutonium's Phonons', January–February 2004, http://www-cms.llnl.gov/s-t/pu-phonons.html; and globalsecurity.org, 'Plutonium Crystal Phase Transitions', n.d., http://www.globalsecurity.org/wmd/intro/pu-phase.htm.

10   The radiation emitted is in the form of alpha particles, which cannot penetrate paper, let alone human skin. However, alpha radiation is carcinogenic if the source is inhaled – the most dangerous route – or ingested. Only a very small range of particle sizes are respirable, however. Both plutonium and uranium are heavy metals and therefore chemically toxic, quite apart from their radioactive qualities. See W.G. Sutcliffe *et al.*, 'A Perspective on the Dangers of Plutonium', Lawrence Livermore National Laboratory, 14 April 1995, http://www.llnl.gov/csts/publications/Sutcliffe.

11   'The Day They Almost Lost Denver', *Bulletin of the Atomic Scientists*, vol. 55, no. 4, July–August 1999, http://www.thebulletin.org/article.php?art_ofn=ja99ackland, pp. 58–65.

12   *Ibid.*

13   Mark *et al.*, 'Can Terrorists Build Nuclear Weapons?', p. 60.

14   'The bare critical mass ("bare crit") of a material at standard density is the critical mass with no neutron reflector present.' J. Carson Mark, 'Explosive Properties of Reactor Grade Plutonium', *Science and Global Security*, vol. 4, 1993, p. 113. The density of plutonium-oxide powder is about 2.3g/cm^3 versus about 11.5g/cm^3 for full crystal density. Amory Lovins, 'Nuclear Weapons and Power-reactor Plutonium', *Nature*, vol. 283, no. 5750, 28 February 1980, http://www.rmi.org/images/other/Security/S80-01_NucWeaponsAndPluto.pdf.

15   Mark *et al.*, 'Can Terrorists Build Nuclear Weapons?', p. 57.

16   Lovins, 'Nuclear Weapons', p. 2.

17   Mark *et al.*, 'Can Terrorists Build Nuclear Weapons?', p. 57.

18   *Ibid.*, p. 59, 61.

19   Under such circumstances, the nuclear yield might be equivalent to no more than the mass of the fissile materials (a few tens of kilograms of TNT). However, it would scatter radioactive matter, some of which would be dangerous isotopes, and thereby be a fairly effective RDD.

20   Carey Sublette, 'Implosion Assembly', Nuclear Weapons Archive, http://nuclearweaponarchive.org/Library/Implsion.html.

21   Mark *et al.*, 'Can Terrorists Build Nuclear Weapons?', p. 62.

22   The term 'trigger' is also used for the fission primary stage of a multistage thermonuclear bomb.

23   US Department of Defense, *Militarily Critical Technologies List (MCTL) Part II: Weapons of Mass Destruction Technologies, Part V: Nuclear Weapons Technology,*

February 1998, http://www.fas.org/irp/threat/mctl98-2/p2sec05.pdf, p. II-5-61.

24 Mark *et al.*, 'Can Terrorists Build Nuclear Weapons?', p. 60.

25 W.J. Frank, 'Preface', in D.A. Dobson *et al.*, 'Summary Report of the Nth Country Experiment', University of California, Livermore, March 1967, http://www.gwu.edu/~nsarchiv/nsa/NC/nh8_4.gif, p. 4.

26 Dan Stober, 'No Experience Necessary', *Bulletin of the Atomic Scientists*, vol. 59, no. 2, March–April 2003, http://www.thebulletin.org/article.php?art_ofn=ma03stober, pp. 56–63.

27 Eugene D. Commins and David A. Dobson, 'Beta-Decay Asymmetry and Nuclear Magnetic Moment of Neon-19', *Physical Review Letters*, 15 April 1963.

28 D. N. Pipkorn *et al.*, 'Mössbauer Effect in Iron under Very High Pressure', *Physical Review Letters*, 14 September 1964.

29 The censored report is reproduced by various websites. It is available as a continuous PDF file from George Washington University's National Security Archive, http://www.gwu.edu/~nsarchiv/news20030701/nth-country.pdf.

30 Stober, 'No Experience Necessary'.

31 *Ibid.*

32 *Ibid.*

33 *Ibid.*

34 Dobson, quoted in *ibid.*

35 *Ibid.*

36 Oliver Burkeman, 'How Two Students Built an A-bomb', *The Guardian*, 24 June 2003, http://www.guardian.co.uk/g2/story/0,3604,983646,00.html.

37 The *Los Alamos Primer* is for sale on Amazon.com. On 21 August 2005, it was retailing for $37.95 after a $2 discount.

38 Allison, *Nuclear Terrorism*, p. 88.

39 The full title of Phillips's thesis was 'An Assessment of the Problems and Possibilities Confronting a Terrorist Group or Non-nuclear Nation Attempting to Design a Crude Pu^{239} Fission Bomb'. *Ibid.*

40 All bomb design data is from Carey Sublette, 'Complete List of All US Nuclear Weapons', Nuclear Weapons Archive, http://nuclearweaponarchive.org/Usa/Weapons/Allbombs.html.

41 Carey Sublette, 'The B61 (Mk-61) Bomb: Intermediate Yield Strategic and Tactical Thermonuclear Bomb', Nuclear Weapons Archive, http://nuclearweaponarchive.org/Usa/Weapons/B61.html.

42 Michael Flynn, 'But Is It Art?', *Bulletin of the Atomic Scientists*, January–February 2004, http://www.thebulletin.org/article.php?art_ofn=jfo4flynn.

43 A photograph reproduced online by the Manhattan Project Heritage Preservation Association (MPHPA) appears to be the one referred to in the *Bulletin*'s article. It can be viewed at http://www.childrenofthemanhattanproject.org/LA/PhotoPages-2/LAP-200.htm.

44 Robert S. Norris, quoted in Flynn, 'But Is It Art?'.

45 Waldo Stumpf, 'Birth and Death of the South African Nuclear Weapons Programme', presentation given at the conference '50 Years after Hiroshima' organised by USPID (Unione Scienziati per il Disarmo), Castiglioncello, Italy, 28 September–2 October 1995, http://www.fas.org/nuke/guide/rsa/nuke/stumpf.htm.

46 US Department of Defense, *Militarily Critical Technologies List*, p. II-5-1.

47 David Albright, 'South Africa and the Affordable Bomb', *Bulletin of the Atomic Scientists*, vol. 50, no. 4, July–August 1994, http://www.thebulletin.org/article.php?art_ofn=ja94albright.

48 European Nuclear Society, 'Uranium Reserves', http://www.euronuclear.org/info/encyclopedia/u/uranium-reserves.htm.

49 Stumpf, 'Birth and Death'.

50 *Ibid.*

51 US Department of Defense, *Militarily Critical Technologies List*, p. II-5-61.

52 *Ibid.*, p. II-5-2.

53 It is reasonable to assume that these three years were spent in research and development, rather than in waiting for a supply of HEU; the first device was built with DU

– it could equally well have been made with natural uranium – so its construction was independent of the enrichment plant's production schedule.

54 See *Global Proliferation of Weapons of Mass Destruction: A Case Study on the Aum Shinrikyo*, Staff Statement, Senate Government Affairs Permanent Subcommittee on Investigations, 31 October 1995, reproduced on the Federation of American Scientists (FAS) website at http://www.fas.org/irp/congress/1995_rpt/aum/index.html); Kyle B. Olson, 'Aum Shinrikyo: Once and Future Threat?', *Emerging Infectious Diseases*, vol. 5, no. 4, July–August 1999, http://www.cdc.gov/ncidod/EID/vol5no4/olson.htm, pp. 513–16; and Jackie Fowler, 'Aum Shinrikyo', *The Religious Movements Homepage Project@The University of Virginia*, religiousmovements.lib.virginia.edu/nrms/aums.html. Factual information on the cult is drawn from these sources, unless otherwise indicated.

55 Gavin Cameron, 'Multi-track Microproliferation: Lessons from Aum Shinrikyo and Al Qa'ida', *Studies in Conflict & Terrorism*, no. 22, 1999, p. 286.

56 *Ibid.*

57 *Ibid.*, p. 287.

58 Sara Daly, John Parachini and William Rosenau, *Aum Shinrikyo, Al Qaeda, and the Kinshasa Reactor: Implications of Three Case Studies for Combating Nuclear Terrorism*, RAND Project Air Force (Santa Monica, CA: RAND Corporation, 2005), p. 14.

59 Matthew Bunn, *The Next Wave: Urgently Needed New Steps To Control Warheads and Fissile Material*, Carnegie Endowment for International Peace and the Harvard Project on Managing the Atom, March 2000, p. 15.

60 Daly, Parachini and Rosenau, *Aum Shinrikyo*, pp. 14–15.

61 Bunn, *The Next Wave*, p. 15.

62 Daly, Parachini and Rosenau, *Aum Shinrikyo*, p. 14.

63 Cameron, 'Multi-track Microproliferation', p. 294.

Chapter Three

1 'Terrorism' here refers primarily to a violent *tactic* that may be adopted in pursuit of a *strategy* by a given group. It is certainly not an ideology, and using terrorism need not define a group as 'terrorist'. While 'terrorism' is typically reserved for the acts of subnational or transnational actors, states can and often do commit terrorism.

2 See, 'Psychotic Murders: Savage Kidnappers Are Holding All Iraq to Ransom', *TimesOnline*, 9 October 2004, http://www.timesonline.co.uk/print-Friendly/0,,1-41-1301013,00.html.

3 Martha Crenshaw, 'The Strategic Logic of Terrorism', in Richard K. Betts (ed.), *Conflict after the Cold War: Arguments on Causes of War and Peace*, 2nd edition (New York: Pearson Longman, 2004), p. 493.

4 Maxwell Taylor and Edith Quayle, *Terrorist Lives* (London: Brassey's, 1994), p. 13.

5 See Jerrold M. Post, 'Terrorist Psycho-logic: Terrorist Behavior as a Product of Psychological Forces', in Walter Reich (ed.), *Origins of Terrorism* (Baltimore, MD: Johns Hopkins University Press, 1998), pp. 25–6.

6 Summarised from the *Diagnostic and Statistical Manual of the American Psychiatric Association, 4th Edition (DSM-IV)*, AllPsych Online, http://allpsych.com/disorders/personality/narcissism.html.

7 Olson, 'Aum Shinrikyo'.

8 Shoko Asahara, speaking on 27 April 1994, quoted in 'III – Background of the Cult', *Global Proliferation of Weapons of Mass Destruction: A Case Study on the Aum Shinrikyo*.

9 Jerrold M. Post, paraphrased in Andrew Maykuth, 'Bin Laden a "Malignant" Personality Who Commands Attention, CIA Expert', *Philadelphia Inquirer*, 10

November 2004, http://www.maykuth. com/stories/terror1110.htm.

10 Bruce Hoffman, quoted in *ibid.*

11 Post, in *ibid.*, p. 35.

12 Post, in *ibid.*, p. 36.

13 Crenshaw, 'The Strategic Logic of Terrorism', p. 498.

14 *Ibid.*, p. 498.

15 *Ibid.*, p. 500.

16 Jerrold M. Post, 'Differentiating the Threat of Radiological/Nuclear Terrorism: Motivations and Constraints', paper pre- pared for presentation to the Conference on Nuclear Terrorism, IAEA, Vienna, 2 November 2001, p. 3. Supplied by the author.

17 Charles D. Ferguson and William C. Potter, *The Four Faces of Nuclear Terrorism* (Monterey, CA: Center for Nonproliferation Studies, 2004), p. 19.

18 Post, 'Differentiating the Threat', p. 5.

19 Paul Arthur, University of Ulster and United States Institute of Peace, quoted on PBS Frontline, 'The IRA and Sinn Fein', http://www.pbs.org/wgbh/pages/ frontline/shows/ira/conflict.

20 Estimates of the human cost of the con- flict vary; see 'Russian Withdrawal', n.d., http://www.globalsecurity.org/military/ world/war/chechnya1-1.htm.

21 Don Radlauer 'An Engineered Tragedy: Statistical Analysis of Casualties in the Palestinian–Israeli Conflict, September 2000–September 2002', International Policy Institute for Counter-Terrorism, 24 June 2002, updated 29 September 2004, www.ict. org.il/articles/articledet.cfm?articleid=439; and Human Rights Watch, 'Israel/Occupied Palestinian Territories', *World Report 2005* (New York/Washington DC: Human Rights Watch, 2005), p. 473. Both sources give a ratio of roughly three Palestinian deaths to every Israeli killed; the ratio of injuries appears to be around five or six to one.

22 Gary Ackerman and Laura Snyder, 'Would They If They Could?', *Bulletin of the Atomic Scientists*, May–June 2002, http://www.thebulletin.org/issues/2002/ mjo2/mjo2ackerman.html.

23 Post, 'Differentiating the Threat', p. 5.

24 Richard A. Falkenrath, Robert D. Newman and Bradley A. Thayer, *America's Achilles' Heel : Nuclear, Biological, and Chemical Terrorism and Covert Attack*, BCSIA Studies in International Security (Cambridge, MA: MIT Press, 1998), p. 194.

25 *Ibid.*, p. 195.

26 Bruce Hoffman, *Inside Terrorism* (London: Victor Gollancz, 1998), p. 88.

27 Centers for Disease Control, 'Disease Information: Salmonellosis: General Information', http://www.cdc.gov/ ncidod/dbmd/diseaseinfo/salmonello- sis_g.htm,

28 'Infection: Infections of Specific Organ Systems: Gastrointestinal Infections: Salmonella', *Encyclopedia Britannica 2004 Standard CD-ROM edition.*

29 John V. Parachini, 'Comparing Motives and Outcomes of Mass Casualty Terrorism Involving Conventional and Unconventional Weapons', *Studies in Conflict & Terrorism*, no. 24, 2001, p. 390.

30 Olson, 'Aum Shinrikyo', p. 514.

31 *Ibid.*

32 *Global Proliferation of Weapons of Mass Destruction: A Case Study on the Aum Shinrikyo.*

33 From Mayer, 'Cults, Violence and Religious Terrorism', pp. 5–10.

34 *Ibid.*, p. 10.

35 Robert Futrell and Barbara G. Brents, 'Protest as Terrorism? The Potential for Violent Anti-Nuclear Activism', *American Behavioral Scientist*, vol. 46, no. 6, February 2003, p. 759.

36 Ferguson and Potter, *The Four Faces of Nuclear Terrorism*, p. 25.

37 This is an unfortunate nomenclature; res- toration ecology is a respectable discipline that concentrates on restoring the natural ecology in areas that have been damaged by human activity or natural disaster.

38 Walter Laqueur, 'Postmodern Terrorism', *Global Issues*, vol. 2, no. 1, February 1997, http://usinfo.state. gov/journals/itgic/0297/ijge/gj-3.htm.

39 *Ibid.*, p. 196.

40 Bin Laden, interview with ABCNews producer Rahimullah Yousafsai, 'Terror Suspect'. The interview was conducted in December 1998, and published on 26 September 2001; http://abcnews.go.com/sectionsworld/DailyNews/transcript_binladen1_981228.html.

41 David Albright, 'Al Qaida's Nuclear Program: Through the Window of Seized Documents', Nautilus Institute Special Forum 47, 6 November 2002, http://www.nautilus.org/fora/Special-Policy-Forum/47_Albright.html#sect2.

42 David Albright, Kathryn Buehler and Holly Higgins, 'Bin Laden and the Bomb', *Bulletin of the Atomic Scientists*, January–February 2002, vol. 58, no. 1, http://www.thebulletin.org/issues/2002/jf02/jf02albright.html, p. 23.

43 See Kimberly McCloud and Matthew Osborne, 'WMD Terrorism and Usama bin Laden', Center for Nonproliferation Studies, n.d., http://cns.miis.edu/pubs/reports/binladen.htm.

44 *Ibid.*

45 *The 9/11 Commission Report: Final Report of the National Commission on Terrorist Attacks Upon the United States*, Official Government Edition (Washington DC: US Government Printing Office, 2004), http://www.gpoaccess.gov/911/pdf/full-report.pdf, p. 172.

46 Dana Priest and Josh White, 'War Helps Recruit Terrorists, Hill Told; Intelligence Officials Talk of Growing Insurgency', *Washington Post*, 17 February 2005, p. A0.

47 CIA, *Unclassified Report to Congress on the Acquisition of Technology Relating to Weapons of Mass Destruction and Advanced Conventional Munitions, 1 July through 31 December 2003*, n.d., http://www.cia.gov/cia/reports/721_reports/july_dec2003.htm.

48 CIA, Directorate of Intelligence, 'Terrorist CBRN: Materials and Effects', CTC 2003-40058, May 2003, http://www.odci.gov/cia/reports/terrorist_cbrn/CBRN_threat.pdf.

49 CIA, *Unclassified Report to Congress on the Acquisition of Technology Relating to Weapons of Mass Destruction and Advanced Conventional Munitions, 1 January through 30 June 2003*, n.d., http://www.cia.gov/cia/reports/721_reports/pdfs/jan_jun2003.pdf.

50 Al Goodman *et al.*, 'Spain Bombs: Moroccan Group Named', *CNN.com*, 30 March 2004, http://www.cnn.com/2004/WORLD/europe/03/30/spain.bombings/index.html.

51 *Ibid.*

52 For an excellent compilation of academic writings on al-Qaeda and source documents by bin Laden and others, see 'The War on Terrorism: Osama bin Laden and al-Qa'ida', Joyner Library Academic Library Services, East Carolina University, http://www.lib.ecu.edu/govdoc/terrorism.html.

53 'A Year after Iraq War: Mistrust of America in Europe Ever Higher, Muslim Anger Persists', Pew Research Center for the People and the Press, 16 March 2004, http://people-press.org/reports/display.php3?ReportID=206. See also 'About this Survey', Pew Research Center, http://people-press.org/reports/display.php3?PageID=797.

54 Al Pessin, 'Pentagon Says Al-Qaida Leader Criticizes Iraq Insurgents', *Voice of America*, 7 October 2005, http://www.globalsecurity.org/military/library/news/2005/10/mil-051007-voa03.htm.

55 'Madrid Remembers Train Bombings', *BBC News World Edition*, 11 March 2005, http://news.bbc.co.uk/2/hi/europe/4338727.stm.

56 Steven Kull, 'War on Terrorism Has Not Made Public Feel Safer', PIPA/Knowledge Networks, 9 September 2003, http://www.pipa.org/OnlineReports/Terrorism/PressRelTerr9.03.pdf; and 'Americans On Terrorism: Two Years after 9/11', PIPA/Knowledge Networks, 9 September 2003, http://www.pipa.org/OnlineReports/Terrorism/FindingsTerr9.03.pdf.

57 Ackerman and Snyder, 'Would They If They Could?'.

58 While bin Laden appears to be knowledgeable of the Koran and is very devout,

he is not a recognised Muslim religious authority, and therefore has no right in Muslim jurisprudence to issue religious edicts, or *fatwas*.

59 Shaykh Usamah Bin-Muhammad Bin-Ladin, Ayman al-Zawahiri, amir [chief or leader] of the Jihad Group in Egypt, Abu-Yasir Rifa'i Ahmad Taha, Egyptian Islamic Group, Shaykh Mir Hamzah, secretary of the Jamiat-ul-Ulema-e-Pakistan, Fazlur Rahman, amir of the Jihad Movement in Bangladesh, 'Jihad Against Jews and Crusaders: World Islamic Front Statement', 23 February 1998, reproduced by the FAS, http://www.fas.org/irp/world/para/docs/980223-fatwa.htm.

60 *Ibid.*

61 *Ibid.*

62 Quintan Wiktorowicz and John Kaltner, 'Killing in the Name of Islam: Al-Qaeda's Justification for September 11', *Middle East Policy Council Journal*, vol. 10, no. 2, Summer 2003, http://www.mepc.org/public_asp/journal_vol10/0306_wiktorowiczkaltner.asp.

63 'A Statement from Qaidat Al-Jihad Regarding the Mandates of the Heroes and the Legality of the Operations in New York and Washington', April 2002, translated by *Middle East Policy Council Journal*.

64 *Ibid.*

65 *Ibid.*

66 Sheik Nasir bin Hamid al Fahd, 'Risalah fi hukm istikhdam aslihat al-damar al-shamel didh al-kuffar' [A Treatise on the Legal Status of Using Weapons of Mass Destruction against Infidels], English translation by the Carnegie Endowment for International Peace, http://www.carnegieendowment.org/static/npp/fatwa.pdf, p. 3.

67 *Ibid.*, p. 9.

68 'Osama bin Laden's Mandate for Nuclear Terror: Al Qaeda Leader Received Religious Justification To Use Weapons of Mass Destruction', Jewish Institute for National Affairs (JINSA), 10 December 2004, http://www.jinsa.org/articles/articles.html/function/view/categoryid/1701/documentid/2762/history/3,2360,655,1701,2762.

69 Ariel Cohen, 'Preventing a Nightmare Scenario: Terrorist Attacks Using Russian Nuclear Weapons and Materials', Backgrounder 1,854, Heritage Foundation, 20 May 2005, http://www.heritage.org/Research/NationalSecurity/bg1854.cfm.

Chapter Four

1 Admiral Richard W. Mies, 'Testimony Before The Senate Armed Services Committee Strategic Subcommittee On Command Posture', 11 July 2001, http://armed-services.senate.gov/statemnt/2001/010711mies.pdf, pp. 4–5.

2 George W. Bush, quoted in Peter Singer, *The President of Good and Evil* (New York: Dutton, 2004), p. 144.

3 David Hughes, 'Uranium Seizures Heighten Terrorism Concerns', *Aviation Week and Space Technology*, 3 April 1995, p. 63, cited in Barry L. Rothberg, 'Note: Averting Armageddon: Preventing Nuclear Terrorism in the United States', *Duke Journal of Comparative & International Law*, vol. 8, no. 1, Autumn 1997, http://www.law.duke.edu/shell/cite.pl?8+Duke+J.+Comp.+&+Int'l+L.+79, p. 125.

4 Rothberg, 'Note', pp. 125–6.

5 See Stan Erickson, 'Nuclear Weapon Prepositioning as a Threat Strategy', *Journal of Homeland Security*, July 2001, http://www.homelandsecurity.org/journal/articles/displayArticle.asp?article=15.

6 Brian M. Jenkins, 'Is Nuclear Terrorism Plausible?', in Leventhal and Alexander (eds), *Preventing Nuclear Terrorism*, p. 33.

7 *Ibid.*, p. 32.

Appendix

1 James L. Ford, 'Radiological Dispersal Devices: Assessing the Transnational Threat', *Strategic Forum*, no. 136, March 1998, http://www.ndu.edu/inss/strforum/SF136/forum136.html.

2 Leonid Bolshov, Rafael Arutunyan and Oleg Pavlovsky, 'Radiological Terrorism', in Committee on Confronting Terrorism in Russia (Sigfried S. Hecker, Chair), *High Impact Terrorism: Proceedings of a Russian–American Workshop* (Washington DC: National Academy Press, 2002), p.141.

3 Charles D. Ferguson, Tahseen Kazi and Judith Perera, *Commercial Radioactive Sources: Surveying the Security Risks*, Occasional Paper 11, Center for Nonproliferation Studies, Monterey Institute for International Studies, January 2003, http://cns.miis.edu/pubs/opapers/op11/op11.pdf, p. 17.

4 *Ibid.*, p. v. The authors also point out that companies may be reluctant to admit to losing radiation sources, so these figures probably under-represent the problem.

5 'Radiological Dispersal Device (RDD)', Argonne National Laboratory, EVS Human Health Fact Sheet, August 2005, http://www.ead.anl.gov/pub/doc/rdd.pdf.

6 Ferguson *et al.*, 'Commercial Radioactive Sources', p. v.

7 Testimony of Dr. Henry Kelly, President, Federation of American Scientists, before the Senate Committee on Foreign Relations, 6 March 2002, http://www.fas.org/ssp/docs/kelly_testimony_030602.pdf.

8 'Radiological Dispersal Device (RDD)'.

9 Ford, 'Radiological Dispersal Devices'.